# Alcoholic Christians

Steven Kopor

AmErica House
Baltimore

Copyright 2001 by Steven Kopor
All rights reserved. No part of this book may be reproduced in any form without written permission from the publishers, except by a reviewer who may quote brief passages in a review to be printed in a newspaper or magazine.

First printing

Author photograph by Art Lederman.

ISBN: 1-58851-508-7
PUBLISHED BY AMERICA HOUSE BOOK PUBLISHERS
www.publishamerica.com
Baltimore

Printed in the United States of America

# TABLE OF CONTENTS

DEDICATION PAGE .............................. 7

ACKNOWLEDGMENT ........................... 9

WE CHRISTIAN ALCOHOLICS ................... 11

A BRIEF HISTORY ON DISEASE THEORY ......... 17
    God's Model .............................. 17
    The Church Initially Rejected the Scientific
    Medical Model ............................ 18
    The Church Accepted the Scientific Medical
    Model ................................... 19
    The Psychiatric and Psychological Model ....... 19
    Science Rejected the Validity of the Christian
    Healing Ministry .......................... 21
    Science Accepted Occult Science ............. 22
    Christians Should Accept Secular Science but
    Reject its Occult Science Components ......... 23
    Alcoholism and Drunkenness are a Primary
    Spiritual Diseases .......................... 24

THE SPIRITUAL CAUSES OF ALCOHOLISM
AND DRUNKENNESS ........................... 27
    Sin: The Forgotten Variable in Drunkenness ..... 29
        Original Sin ........................ 29
        Personal Sin ....................... 31
        Gluttony .......................... 35
        The Sin Complex of Drunks ........... 36
        Enabling is a Sin ................... 38
    Fallen Angel's: The Forgotten Variable in
    Drunkenness ............................. 38
        Demonic Aggression ................. 39
        The Demonic Personality-Know Your
        Enemy ........................... 40

Direct Demonic Influence . . . . . . . . . . . . . 42
　　　Temptation . . . . . . . . . . . . . . . . . . . . . . . . 44
　　　Generational Curses . . . . . . . . . . . . . . . . . 45
　　　Why Demons Possess . . . . . . . . . . . . . . . . 49

THE PROGRESSION OF THE SPIRITUAL DISEASE . 51
　　How Progression Takes Place . . . . . . . . . . . . . . . . 52
　　Formation of Vice . . . . . . . . . . . . . . . . . . . . . . . . . 55
　　Alcoholics Learn to be Helpless . . . . . . . . . . . . . . 56
　　Alcoholics Become Defensive . . . . . . . . . . . . . . . . 57
　　Destruction of the Conscience . . . . . . . . . . . . . . . . 59
　　Alcohol Induced Disorders of the Will . . . . . . . . . 62
　　　　Inability to Perceive God's Will . . . . . . . . . 63
　　　　Opposition to God's Will . . . . . . . . . . . . . . 63
　　　　Inability to Accomplish God's Will . . . . . . 64
　　　　Confusing God's Will with the Demonic
　　　　Will and Self Will . . . . . . . . . . . . . . . . . . . 65
　　　　Willpower Weakness . . . . . . . . . . . . . . . . . 65
　　Psychosomatic Manifestations . . . . . . . . . . . . . . . . 69
　　Alcoholics with Psychiatric Disorders . . . . . . . . . . 70
　　The Churches Complicity in Progression . . . . . . . 71

RELAPSE PREVENTION . . . . . . . . . . . . . . . . . . . . . . . 75
　　The Spiritual Steps to Relapse . . . . . . . . . . . . . . . . 76
　　　　The First Step: The Temptation . . . . . . . . . 77
　　　　The Second Step: Meditation on the
　　　　Temptation . . . . . . . . . . . . . . . . . . . . . . . . . 78
　　　　The Third Step: Deciding in the Heart . . . 79
　　　　The Fourth Step: The Lapse or Relapse . . . 80
　　Changing the Natural Progression of Alcoholism . 80
　　Prevention of the Sin of Drunkenness . . . . . . . . . . 82
　　　　Restrictions on Demons . . . . . . . . . . . . . . . 83
　　　　Unregenerated Human Character . . . . . . . . 84
　　　　Christian Character . . . . . . . . . . . . . . . . . . 85
　　　　Evangelism to the Drunken Alcoholic . . . . 86
　　　　Training Children to be Sober Adults . . . . 86
　　　　Preventing Occasions of Sin . . . . . . . . . . . 87
　　　　Protection From the Sins of Others . . . . . . 88

    Sins of the Scientific Health Professionals  89
    Alcoholic's Must Avoid All Forms
    of Hypnotism ....................... 89

✓ THE DRY DRUNK SYNDROME ................. 93
    The Development of the Dry Drunk ........... 93
    The Dry Drunk's Spiritual Attachment to Alcohol  97
    Dry Drunks are Sober for Worldly,
    Not Spiritual Reasons ..................... 98
    Dry Drunks Practice Idolatry ................ 99
    Dry Drunks Have a Psychological Awakening,
    Not a Spiritual Awakening ................. 100
    The Dry Drunk's Recovery is Based on Works,
    Not Faith .............................. 102
    Dry Drunks Experience Behavioral not
    Spiritual Change ......................... 103
    Dry Drunks are Spiritual but Not Religious ..... 105
    Dry Drunks are Hypersensitive to the Pain
    of Recovery ............................ 108

THE SACRED SCIENCE OF RECOVERY
FROM ALCOHOL ............................ 113
    Preparation for the Reign of Jesus Christ ...... 113
    Christian Recovery ....................... 114
    Intervention of Grace ..................... 116
    Spiritual Exercises for Spiritual Warfare ....... 120
        Important Reasons for Combining
        Religion With Spirituality ............ 121
        The Value of Bible Reading for Recovery  124
        Types of Prayer Important to Alcoholics . 128
        Why Fasting is Especially Important
        to Alcoholics ..................... 134
        Improve Recovery by the Examination
        of the Conscience .................. 136
        Christian Meditation ................ 137
    The Spiritually Sober Alcoholic ............. 139
        Understanding How to Truly Forgive ... 139
        The Acquisition of Virtue ........... 142

> The Pursuit of Christian Perfection ..... 145
> Surrender-Cooperation with Grace ..... 147
> Serenity: The Peace of God ........... 150

THE HOLY SPIRIT EMPOWERED CHRISTIAN
SPONSOR ..................................... 155
    The Best Type of Sponsor ................. 155
    Sponsoring the Non Christian .............. 156
    The Danger of Non Christian Sponsors ........ 156
    Knowledge Versus Discernment Based
    Diagnosis .............................. 158
        Human Nature ..................... 160
        Sin .............................. 162
        Guilt ............................ 162
        Forgiveness ...................... 163
    Treatment for Supernatural Generational Curses . 164
    Counseling a Backslider ................... 166
    Deliverance ............................ 166
    Counseling the Alcoholic for Death, Judgment
    and Eternity ........................... 168

EPILOGUE .................................... 171

# DEDICATION PAGE

This Book is Dedicated to Jesus Christ of Bethlehem

# ACKNOWLEDGMENT

It was only through God's grace, patience and mercy that this book was completed. Therefore, it is appropriate that I acknowledge and thank God, who has been generous to me, his servant. Thank you Lord.

Deep thanks to my wife, Betsy. She walked beside me every step of the way. Her love, support, and collaboration were a blessing.

# WE CHRISTIAN ALCOHOLICS

The grace of our Lord Jesus Christ, the fellowship of the Holy Spirit and the blessings of God the Father be with you, and abundantly with those who read this book. This book on spiritual progress is directed to the poor soul whose only guiding light is that light emitted by hell's fire. It focuses on the process of transforming the drunkard, who is a creature of darkness, into a creature of light.

The road that the drunkard must follow to accomplish spiritual progress is similar to the road that other grave sinners must follow. But the sin of drunkenness is uniquely different from other grave sins because a mind-altering drug is consumed. Therefore, the alcoholic faces unique perils on the road to spiritual progress. This book focuses on the unique battles associated with conversion from drunkenness. Let's not forget that demons know the drunkard's weakness, so it is an uphill battle on the road of Christian recovery and spiritual progress. The hazards are uniquely tailored by the demons to make the drunkard continue in his drunken folly or if the drunkard achieves abstinence, to keep him miserable and set him up for a relapse. The purpose of this book is to show the alcoholic how to have a holy, serene, productive, sober life amid all the spiritual perils unique to recovery.

There are three roads the drunkard can follow. The worst is continued drunkenness, which leads to hell. This road is filled with self-indulgence, selfishness, lust, gluttony, and pain. The second road is the road traveled by the dry drunk. This is a life of contradictions, pain, anguish, misery, despair, and helplessness. The personality of the dry drunk is identical to that of the drunkard, except the dry drunk does not have the sedative effects of alcohol to soothe his aching mind and emotions. The dry drunk has merely stopped drinking. They are not in recovery. The dry drunk lifestyle, although painful, is not always sinful. From the Father's point of view, drunkenness is the sin for which healing and forgiveness is required. Despite the dry drunk's degree of sin, their quality of life is immensely better when compared to the drunkard.

The third road is the road of Christian recovery. God holds out many different methods for the alcoholic to live a happy sober life, but the smoothest road, with fewest detours and obstacles is Jesus Christ.

Drunkenness must be overcome. Once the drunken alcoholic transforms into an abstinent alcoholic, his first step on the road to Christian recovery has begun. With God's nurturing and the alcoholic's own cooperation, the spiritual life of the Christian alcoholic proceeds through the cyclical growth and pruning process. Healing takes place from glory to glory. The alcoholic loses his attachment to drunkenness and begins to seek a closer union with God, to be a better spiritual bride and to be more in Jesus' image and likeness. The recovering Christian alcoholic who is serious about continuous sobriety must come to terms with the reality that recovery depends on continuous spiritual development. They must also learn that without continued sobriety they will probably relapse. The recovering Christian alcoholic cannot accomplish recovery without spiritual progress.

Much of the Christian alcoholic's initial spiritual growth revolves around relapse and abstinence issues. Eventually, the alcohol-specific spiritual issues will lessen and more core spiritual issues will become the battle line for spiritual warfare. They will always be vulnerable to drunkenness but the obstacles to spiritual progress are no longer specific to drunkenness but to the Christian life in general.

Since Adam blamed Eve and Eve blamed the serpent (Genesis 3:12-13) Man has taken undue solace in shirking responsibility for his actions. In the Old Testament murderers received capital punishment regardless of whether a disease caused them to kill. This judgment did not consider mitigating circumstances, excuses, reasons, or justifications. God holds drunks accountable for their sin. In the New Testament it states that drunks will not get into heaven (1 Corinthians 6:9-10). Since God does not send souls to hell for things they are not responsible for, the alcoholic must have some control over whether they become drunk.

There is a very thin line that separates social drinking from drunkenness. The ability to correctly determine this line is very difficult even for the highly skilled substance abuse counselor. How can a chronic drunk ever hope to correctly define this line? Mortal man cannot accurately determine the definition of what qualifies as sinful drunkenness. Even in extreme cases mortal man cannot declare with one hundred percent certainty the sinfulness of a drunken episode. For example, two people could be at a party and be equally intoxicated; yet one willfully decided to get drunk, while the other accidentally drank too much. God, who can separate spirit from soul, bone from marrow, and faith from works, clearly perceives and judges each and every time the line is crossed. On Judgement Day there will be many occasions when the drinker's opinion differs from God's true judgment. Although alcohol is not intrinsically evil, demons make especially good use of its properties to damn mankind. It is because of the ease with which mankind is damned by its use, and the ease with which many drinkers cross the line and become sinfully drunk that alcoholics in recovery should abstain.

Alcoholics and drunks are not exactly the same thing. A person who occasionally drinks and gets drunk is not an alcoholic. He is simply a person who got drunk. Anyone can get drunk if he drinks enough. Therefore, a drunk may or may not be an alcoholic. To merit the name of the vice, the act must be chronic and progressive. When a drunk repents after twenty years of drinking he is no longer a drunk but a sincere virtuous penitent. Nevertheless he is still an alcoholic. The demonic claws are so deeply clenched that he will always be an alcoholic. An alcoholic can be sober or drunk. On the surface, the drinking behavior of the alcoholic does not appear different than that of a non-alcoholic getting drunk. But below the surface, there is something much different which motivates them. It is much more complex than subconscious motivation or an addicted personality. It is a bona fide disease.

To the drunk, the passing pleasures of the material world are elevated far beyond their worth. True eternal values are second place to worldly pleasures. When a drunk is willing to sacrifice eternal glory, it is exceptional depravity. But the drunk is unique even among those who love the world. Their frame of mind is so sick they would voluntarily give up all the world has to offer-wealth, fame, etc.-for the next drink. They accept something with no true value and willingly trade Heaven away.

Some drunks defer abstinence into the indefinite future while others continuously defer it until the next day. Some admit it is too hard for them to quit. Others honestly admit they do not care enough about God, their families, or themselves to exert the necessary effort. They presume on God's mercy and think that God did not mean it when He said that drunks would not inherit the kingdom of God. Others presume they will live until the time they can actually repent. The demons will allow man to experience many delusions in order to keep them under their control through drunkenness. How many have died unexpectedly without advance warning? Many have died and gone to hell because of these false hopes.

Urge within yourself the desire for reconciliation with God and spiritual progress. Do not delay another day! You may wake up tomorrow with a hangover and learn that Christ came during the night and left you behind. When this happens a small remnant of drunkards will repent and bitterly cry the rest of their lives. But for most, there will not be enough alcohol, even if the entire sea were alcohol, to drown their deadly pain. Turn your life around now! Repent today, because tomorrow you could trip over your own drunken feet, die, and go to hell forever. How deluded the poor drunkard who thinks he can fly with angels when in reality he could drown in his own vomit. When you choose to walk on the road to hell, God lets you go to hell. You may not agree with this but it is the truth. The blood of Christ does not cover those who reject Him. The drunk is a living testimony of rejection. The drunk must realize that while he is drinking many souls are burning in hell for drunkenness. Any drunk burning in hell will testify to the importance of sobriety, if only he could. But would a drunk listen?

In Luke 5:31-32, Jesus said, "It is not the healthy who need a doctor, but the sick. I have not come to call the righteous, but sinners to repentance." He was talking about the spiritual illnesses of man. He stated sinners need a healer. Sin should be treated and cured just as any other illness. This book will help treat and God willing, cure the alcoholic, heal his personality, and restore his broken family relationships.

# A BRIEF HISTORY ON DISEASE THEORY

## God's Model

The history of the cause of disease began thousands of years ago with spiritual explanations. Disease was viewed as either a punishment or trial from God, demons, or one of the many false gods. In those days nobody knew the psychological or biological explanations. The church's monasteries were the first hospitals, which provided food, shelter and care for the sick. They also applied supernatural methods. Sometimes miracles were performed, but they always prayed for the sick. They were a visible expression of the Christian healing ministry. Even though modern hospitals are increasingly severed from official church bodies, what other private business has a chaplain and chapel? Today's hospitals are the meeting place for minister, physician, and patient.

Models of healing and illness have changed numerous times throughout history. This is because models are defined by the way a society, its dominant institutions, and the experts in those dominant institutions perceive and explain reality. God's model of healing and illness has remained constant since He is the same yesterday, today and forever. He gave His church great power and authority over illness. Jesus has historically used the prophet, priest, minister, pastor, and faith healer to minister healing. The Bible teaches that the church was given a healing ministry. God continues to minister healing through His body, the church.

## The Church Initially Rejected the Scientific Medical Model

When science entered the stream of time the Catholic Church was the only church. The Protestant communions did not exist yet. The Catholic Church initially rejected the scientific model of medicine for many reasons. The church did not believe the new ideas which science proposed. Illness could not be caused by natural phenomena like viruses or bacteria, because it was always believed to be caused by supernatural spiritual agents (God or demons). The church believed that its healing methods were superior to the scientific methods. In those days the technology of medical science used leeches. The church continued to encourage its members to rely on the established church methods because scientific methods demonstrated a lack of faith.

The church always accepted battlefield surgery, but science wanted to dissect the bodies of deceased humans for research purposes. Battlefield surgery involved the sanctity of life, but dissection for research was considered unclean. Dissection for the advancement of knowledge was unacceptable to the ecclesiastical policy makers. The church passed laws prohibiting dissection. In the 1300's, the Roman Catholic Church's grip on secular society lessened and human dissection became common. This opened the door to the scientific healing practices, because priests would not be morticians. Could you imagine any modern minister who, after administering the sacraments would be interested in going elbow deep in cadavers? He would be Pastor Frankenstein.

## The Church Accepted the Scientific Medical Model

As time went on, the church began to accept the findings of science. Over the centuries, scientists have learned about the germs, viruses, bacteria, etc., which cause illness. Chains of causation include genetic, environmental and social agents. They have also learned many of the different ways which illness is transmitted. The church did not reject its supernatural model, but when evidence became overwhelming, it accepted the scientific model's explanation. It currently embraces both the supernatural model and the natural model in its understanding of diagnosis and treatment. The prominence of the physician arose when the western church accepted the medical model.

## The Psychiatric and Psychological Model

The church had less difficulty accepting the psychiatric and psychological model than it did accepting the scientific medical models because the culture was already desensitized. The world view had changed from the religious to the secular and scientific. Science had already proven itself as a valid healing method. The church had become much more open to scientific advancement, especially within the healing arts, because hundreds of years of conflict had already been resolved.

The psychiatric model convinced the world that the brain was the seat of the mind, will and emotions. This gave them a legitimate and logical reason to treat psychopathology. They claimed that mental diseases were caused by neurological and biochemical factors only. Later the psychologists proclaimed that disease was also caused by psychological factors such as stress, anxiety, shame, guilt, etc. They usurped yet another area of healing which historically belonged to the clergy. When psychiatrists try to cure the soul, they often rely on the pharmacist to cover over rather than cure. If the psychiatrists would have stayed in their field of study (which was medicine, specifically the nervous system) and not usurped the true physicians of the soul, the psychiatric model would be in God's will. When psychiatrists and psychologists claimed to be able to practice what is objectively the cure of the soul, they stepped out of God's will.

Over the course of six centuries, science usurped Christian ministers who are the true physicians of the soul. The cure of souls, confession of sin and biblical counsel became secular scientific therapy. When scientific therapy attempts to replace biblical counsel, you can be sure that demons are involved. Demonically empowered revisionists re-evaluated the ancient medical and psychological literature and determined that it reflected primitive man's naive understanding. Demonically possessed persons were rediagnosed as having multiple personality disorders, epilepsy, or a psychosis. Sins became crimes (stealing, murder) or a disease (drunkenness). Miraculous cures were replaced by spontaneous remission. In hell there must be a book of synonyms which has a scientific word to describe and explain away every spiritual manifestation and treatment. From this demonic book of synonyms, elaborate theories were constructed in which spiritual activity was reinterpreted as psychological and biological phenomena. Demons must laugh at all the sophisticated diagnoses that scientific clinicians have devised to describe illnesses directly caused by them. These new terms are only euphemisms, which describe very old spiritual disorders.

## Science Rejected the Validity of the Christian Healing Ministry

As sick people began to accept science, the physicians were not gracious to the church. Not only did they embrace the natural model, but they rejected the church's supernatural explanations. Therefore the church rejected them. The church's rejection of science's new discoveries was not done in spite. It could not condone the ghoulish practices of medical research. In addition, the medical model claimed that disease was not caused by supernatural beings but by natural causes alone. The church has always asserted that there are spiritual causes of illness, yet there is no scientific evidence. To the church, science's rejection of their supernatural model was heresy. In truth, science merely discovered the natural mechanisms that spiritual agents used to cause illness.

Science rejected the Christian supernatural model and embraced the natural model. It rejected the premise that supernatural factors caused illness. Science continues to reject the spiritual causes of disease. Science and religion have become two distinct methods for the diagnosis and treatment of disease.

Satan caused a change in the ministers of healing through the skillful manipulation of people and circumstances. Satan began planting seeds of hell that would germinate, sprout, grow, and bear fruit over a six hundred year period. A new type of healer would arise. These healers would further separate man from God. The group with authority slowly changed from God's minister to the secular scientific healers. Satan has lived many centuries and used time to his advantage. The world was deceived because Satan implemented the transition very slowly. If Satan had tried to implement the transition quickly, the church would have rebuked him. Satan has worked long and hard over the centuries to accomplish this transition and he will fight to keep things the way he likes them.

Christianity's validation of healing and illness became dependent on science because science became the accepted authority. Centuries earlier, the clergy ruled out a spiritual illness before a patient was referred to the physician. Then the process reversed. Initially the church allowed secular scientific healers to rule out physical illness before they intervened. Soon, society mandated it. This gave Satan the foothold he wanted.

## Science Accepted Occult Science

The occult model consists of Satan's strategies to promote disease in man's spirit, soul, and body. From Satan's point of view, the purpose of scientific healers are to lessen man's dependence on God and His church, to create an opportunity for the spread of occult healing, and to establish a system which would ultimately be responsible for the death of millions, through abortion and euthanasia. All this separated the sick from the healing grace of God.

As a counterfeit to God's healing ministry, demons subtly encourage the use of the occult through new age medicine, psychiatry, and psychology. They also implement healing through the psychic healer and witch doctor. Demons motivate the fraudulent faith healers. They also cause man to take actions that lower his capacity to resist further illnesses.

Today, occult science cloaks itself with new age and scientific terminology, but it is a satanic system designed to infiltrate the world. It applies occult philosophies and practices to healing. Entrapments such as psychic energy, after-death experiences, reincarnation, and hypnotism have become interwoven with the scientific, medical, psychiatric, and psychological models as well as with its professionals.

Through the secular scientific model Satan has transformed the healing professions into the religion of the godless. Science is so busy taking God out of healing that the occult theories and techniques came in the back door. Today many scientific healers are unknowingly involved with demons. Although the scientific model rejects religion, its practitioners are actually saying they want no ties with God's religion but that they are very interested in Satan's religion. The ancient Babylonians said that if a man did not have God, demons cover him like clothes. This is applicable to many scientific healers because they rejected God and the void was quickly filled with demons. The scientific healers have made great advances in their craft over the last few centuries. They have also made great advances in spreading the occult. Before the rise of scientific healers there were only two camps: God's or Satan's. There was a clear distinction. But now the scientific healers blur that distinction since they often incorporate bits of natural and occult science.

## Christians Should Accept Natural Science but Reject Its Occult Science Components

Today physicians apply the scientific model and ministers apply the supernatural model. Both have the same goal but practice different methods. Science focuses on the biological and psychological causes of illness. The church focuses on the biological, psychological, as well as spiritual causes of illness. It is not the medical interventions of the physician or the spiritual interventions of the minister that heal. Jesus is the only source of all healing. Treatment not prescribed by Jesus is dangerous.

Some Christians condemn the scientific methods, rejecting its natural science components along with the occult science. They are not using discernment or good judgment.

The Bible does not state that medicine or psychology is ungodly. In fact, the Gospel according to Luke and the Acts of the Apostles were written by a physician. The natural science aspects are another instrument the Holy Spirit uses to heal the biological and psychological manifestations of demonic aggression. God grants wisdom to his healers and they are at liberty to draw methods and techniques from any source He allows. This includes scientific methods but prohibits occult methods.

When a person becomes ill they should seek the help of an appropriate healer, be it dentist, physician, counselor, church elder, or faith healer. They should go to the minister of healing that God and common sense lead them to through prayerful consideration.

## Alcoholism and Drunkenness Are Primary Spiritual Diseases

The proof that alcoholism and drunkenness are spiritual diseases does not lie in the fact that spiritual treatments cure them because spiritual treatments can also cure physical and psychological diseases. The proof rests in that purely psychological or physical treatments do not work. The suffering from alcoholism and drunkenness can be relieved only by Christian intervention.

The spiritual disease is the first in order of time and development. It is the original condition that is not subordinate to any other cause or condition. It is the cause without which biological and psychological diseases could not occur. The biological and psychological diseases are second in time order, but they do not occupy a subordinate position. Once established, they become independent and appear primary in terms of everything except the order of development.

Alcoholism is not the result of some other disease; it is primary, and causes other diseases.

Scientists need to look beyond natural explanations and see the spiritual disease as primary. They claim that the spiritual causes of alcoholism are a myth. The real myth is that alcoholism is a biological or psychological disease devoid of spiritual causes. The physical and psychological causes that science "discovered" were actually instituted by God as a consequence to Adam's sin.

Who has God's authority to treat alcoholism? Is it the physician, psychologist, or minister? Modern society dictates that medical problems must be treated by a physician, and psychological problems by a psychologist. Since science is impotent in the treatment of sin; drunkenness, a sin, is outside the purview of the scientist. Circumstances place the treatment of drunkenness into the hands of the minister, Christian sponsor, spiritual director, or Christian counselor.

Because science does not view spiritual factors as a cause of illness, a drunk goes from Doctor of Medicine to Doctor of Psychology without ever getting a referral to a Doctor of Divinity, pastor, or Christian counselor, with the gift of healing. It would certainly be a leap in faith for a Christian University to institute a faith healing curriculum.

Because alcoholism is a disease of the spirit it is uniquely disposed to ruin souls. In the supernatural realm its consequences are more grave than mere physical death, since it is sufficient to send a soul to the second death. The second death-that of being thrown into the lake of fire-is the fate of all those who live the lifestyle of a drunk. The drunk experiences hell on earth and will spend eternity in hell.

# THE SPIRITUAL CAUSES OF ALCOHOLISM AND DRUNKENNESS

A combination safe has many possible number sequences, but only the correct combination will open the safe. Likewise, only the correct combination of causal factors will activate alcoholism. Multiple causes in the correct order are necessary. To illustrate, a headache may be caused by a hangover, trauma to the head, stress, a toxin, a virus, high blood pressure, or reading without glasses. The headache can be caused by only one or any combination of potential causes. Sometimes stress alone is insufficient, but stress combined with high blood pressure, which by itself is also insufficient, combines to cause a headache. Therefore, not every alcoholic becomes a drunk when exposed to identical causes. The variation in causal factors is as unique as each drunk. The disease of alcoholism has multiple causes: primarily spiritual, secondarily biological, psychological, and environmental factors.

People are born with a different mix of predispositions to alcoholism. Not everybody is born with the predisposition to alcoholism, but all drunks are. Long before the drunk ever had their first drink, the predisposition to that particular sin lay dormant. The predisposition alone is insufficient, but when combined with peer pressure, for example, which by itself is also insufficient, the disease is activated. The predisposition to alcoholism does not always manifest itself in drunkenness because the things that happen after birth can prevent its activation. For example, the Christian's spiritual, psychological, and physiological predispositions are much different than those of the non-Christian. Conversion imprints a new mix of predispositions on the spirit and soul. Even the probability of getting certain physical illnesses decrease after conversion because many unhealthy behaviors are replaced by

Godly behaviors. The seriousness of alcoholism lies in the strong predisposition to become a drunk, but it is only a predisposition, not predestination.

There are two types of predisposing causes. First, there are predispositions, which are part of man's nature since the fall of Adam. For example, all humans are predisposed to illness, sin, and other demonic aggression. The second type of predisposition resides under the umbrella of individual differences. These predispositions are not common to all mankind, but vary from person to person because of genetics, generational curses, environment factors, etc. Not everyone is predisposed to alcoholism.

The disease theory is misapplied when it exonerates the drunkard from personal responsibility. It dishonestly reduces their guilt and remorse. These judgmental processes are the natural consequences of their sinful behavior and can be a catalyst for early recovery. Seeing the guilt of drunkenness is a great gift and demonstrates that the light of the Holy Spirit is shining on the drunk's conscience. The belief that drunkenness is devoid of personal responsibility is counterproductive to true spiritual recovery. They must become free by God's forgiveness not by erroneous rationalization. Recovery based on delusion is as a foundation built on sand.

Diseases like cancer or diabetes can destroy the body or mind, but the spirit is not damaged. This is because disease is amoral or spiritually neutral. A person could have the disease of cancer, not sin, die and go to Heaven. Or, they could have the disease of cancer, reason, "what the hell" and continuously commit heinous sins until they die and go to hell. Likewise, the disease of alcoholism has no bearing on one's eternal resting place. God does not send souls to hell for alcoholism; He sends them there for drunkenness. Alcoholism is a disease but drunkenness is a character flaw. The disease of alcoholism can be a test from God but active drunkenness is never a test, it is a complete rejection of God.

# Sin: The Forgotten Variable in Drunkenness

## Original Sin

Man's soul was created with the predisposition to spiritual error as is evidenced by his decision to commit original sin. If man's spirit did not have the predisposition to sin, Adam could not have sinned. Without a predisposing cause, no one could get a disease.

God originally made mankind in His image and likeness. Because of Adam's sin all his progeny would be cut from a different mold than he. Man is also born in the image of fallen Adam (Genesis 5:3). His descendants would be born more and more in his (Adam's) image and likeness. Within a few generations the demonic influence increased so much that man appeared more satanic than Godly. Man became so corrupt that God regretted that He created man. Therefore, He sent the flood.

Much of what Adam lost, Jesus, through his death and resurrection restored, but while on earth mankind will never be completely restored to the original intention of God. The physical and psychological effects of original sin will be a part of man's makeup until death do they part. Original sin caused God to implement a punishment. Therefore, the consequences of original sin are God's will.

The consequences of Adam's original sin include: God placed a curse on mankind; man became a fallen creature and lost sovereignty over the world, became afraid of God, learned to avoid accountability, was banished from the Garden of Eden; nakedness was perceived as wrong; and death, illness and a propensity to commit actual sin became second nature.

Original sin took power away from the human soul. It damaged the mind, will, and emotions. It converted man's soul from pure and wholesome to being cluttered with much perversity.

It would be an understatement to say that the demonic influence over man exponentially increased. Original sin allowed the demons greater authority and control over mankind's mind, will, emotions, and body to shape mankind into their own demonic image. Original sin is responsible, either directly or indirectly, for all human misery. This means that without original sin, illness would never have entered the stream of time. Without original sin there would be no disease, including alcoholism. Original sin created the original spiritual disease which is the context for all sin and disease, not merely drunkenness and addiction. Alcoholism's root cause is spiritual and proceeds directly from original sin. It is reinforced by personal sin. The spiritual disease can manifest itself through thousands of forms besides alcoholism.

The most grievous effect of man's original sin was the relational shift between God, man, and Satan. Satan acquired what he had previously coveted, which was sovereignty over the Earth. Satan can boldly say that he is "the prince of this world," (John 12:31, 14:30, 16:11); "the ruler of the kingdom of the air," (Ephesians 2:2); and "the god of this age," (2 Corinthians 4:4). The temptation of Jesus by Satan (Luke 4:5-7) demonstrates Satan's sovereignty over the world. Jesus did not dispute Satan's statement of legal authority to rule over the world.

Original sin severely disturbed man's mind because he ate from the tree of knowledge. Knowledge became a predominant part of man's mind, instead of faith.

## Personal Sin

Original sin established the precedent. It opened a gate through which all of Adam's descendants must walk. Adam's original sin brought death, illness, sin, and demonic possession into the world. Personal sin nourishes it. Personal sin occupies much of the mind's time whether it is involved in planning, doing, or resisting sin.

Personal sin is to original sin as water is to mortal life. Personal sin is a personal act of rebellion against God's holy will. It is the surrendering of the will to Satan. The demons are the only creatures that rejoice over the drunk's sin. Through actual sin the drunk's mind becomes open to all sorts of demonic influence.

Sin is transmuted into physical, psychological, detectable, undetectable, temporal, and ephemeral phenomena (Deuteronomy 28:15-35, 59-61). God allows powerful delusions (2 Thessalonians 2:11) blindness of mind (2 Corinthians 4:3-4) and guilt and shame as a consequence to sin. Guilt and shame each have psychological and somatic manifestations.

Sometimes there is an obvious correlation between a sin and its consequence. For example, obesity is often caused by gluttony, and sexually transmitted disease by fornication or adultery. Sometimes the correlation is less obvious. There are manifestations of sin that are below the threshold of human perception. The damaging effects of drunkenness do not always appear related to drinking.

### Mortal Versus Venial Sin

Biblically, sin can be classified according to its severity: mortal and venial sin. 1 John 5:16-17 states, "If anyone sees his brother commit a sin that does not lead to death, he should pray and God will give him life. I refer to those whose sin does not lead to death. There is a sin that leads to death..."

Sin is called deadly sin, mortal sin, or grave sin because its commission immediately kills any accumulated grace in the soul. A person does not have to commit two or more mortal sins to merit hell, one is sufficient. It is mortal sin that Jesus describes when he says that some will say to Him, "But did not I cast out demons and raise the dead in your name," and He said, "I do not know you." Very serious sin is likened to a mortal wound, which leads to physical death. A mortal sin wounds the soul in such a grave way that after physical death the second death is guaranteed. Since mortal sin destroys the soul's grace, the sinner is plagued with more psychological and/or physiological illness. This means that people could do good things and have them count for very little because they do them when guilty of mortal sin. The poor drunk-guilty of mortal sin upon mortal sin. Their conscience becomes dead. They begin not to care that it is a sin. Soon they do not care to repent.

Venial sin does not completely separate a soul from God, as does mortal sin. It does not destroy all accumulated grace as does mortal sin, but it seriously damages it. The soul's vigor, resilience, strength, and energy level are greatly lessened. It reduces the soul's ability to receive grace and causes it to act in ways that prevent the alcoholic from manifesting grace in the world. The danger in venial sin is that it encourages the demons to cause more temptation and it increases the sinner's chances of committing a mortal sin. Even when venial sin does not end in mortal sin, it weakens the drunk's will, blinds the mind with defense mechanisms like denial, and perverts the emotions.

There are ministers who say a sin is a sin and that when the least of the law is broken the entire law is broken. That statement proclaims the letter of the law. God is the writer of the law and it is He who judges righteously with mercy. He knows the difference between a man who steals food to feed his starving family and a man who is a drunk. Each incurs a different amount of guilt. The thoughts of the mind, the attractions of the will, and the sentiments of the emotions are different between the man who steals to feed his family and the drunk. True, both have violated a commandment and fallen short of God's glory. The drunk would not inherit the Kingdom of God. The man who steals food to feed his starving family, only God knows.

It has been said that Christians are the light of the world. Venial sin lowers the light's brightness. Drunkenness, a mortal sin, extinguishes the light.

### Active Versus Passive Sin

The similarity between a "sin of action" versus "a passive sin of omission" is that both acts are contrary to God. Both are violations of conduct. Sins of action occur when a person actively gets drunk, steals, murders, etc. They did something they should not have done. A sin of omission occurs when the drunk fails to fulfill a divine obligation. Leaving good undone is a sin of omission. Drunks are notorious for not fulfilling their divine obligation to properly raise their children, love their spouse, and not getting the help they need to begin recovery. For the alcoholic in recovery, missing church or Alcoholics Anonymous meetings are sins of omission. The alcoholic must do these good things to remain sober. Avoiding them is a sin because it is giving in to the devil's temptations. It is a failure to do something they should do.

## Deliberate Versus Unintentional Sin

Sin can be committed deliberately or unintentionally (Leviticus 4:13). Deliberate sins are committed when the perpetrator has complete freedom of will and possesses full knowledge of the behavior's sinful nature. The compulsive liar may unconsciously lie and never realize he lied. He did not plan to lie but did it compulsively. Because of some psychopathology or short circuit in his thought process the compulsive liar is less responsible. They are literally retarded in that soul process. In this isolated area they have not reached moral accountability, while in other life areas they are full functioning adults. Even when the sin is unconsciously compelled, as is much drunkenness, the person is still responsible for the sin.

## Conditional Sin

Some behaviors only become sins under certain conditions. The behavior itself is not intrinsically sinful, nor does it intrinsically merit guilt. For example, sex is not intrinsically a sin. It becomes a sin when performed outside of marriage. Drinking alcohol is not intrinsically a sin. It becomes a sin when the drinker gets drunk. When the alcoholic drinks, but does not get drunk, no sin occurred, but it is playing with hell's fire.

## Blaspheming the Holy Spirit

There is a type of sin that is so grave, so mortal, that it is unforgivable. It is called blaspheming the Holy Spirit (Matthew 12-31). Satan and the other demons are the only creatures the Bible illustrates as having blasphemed the Holy Spirit. A satanic high priest that murders and gets drunk could repent, accept Jesus Christ as Lord, and rejoice in the House of the Lord for eternity. Obviously, he did not meet the criteria for blaspheming the Holy Spirit since he was moved to repentance and restored to God's grace. This does not detract from the very grave nature of his behavior. If he were to die with his sins unrepented he would burn in hell forever. In order for a drunk to blaspheme the Holy Spirit, he must die with no remorse for his drunkenness.

**Gluttony**

It is common knowledge that there are seven deadly sins. They are: lust, gluttony, sloth, covetousness, anger, envy, and pride. All sins factor down to these seven deadly sins, and pride is the common denominator of the seven. Is it any wonder that pride is at the root of all the sins in creation? Pride was the cause of both the angels' rebellion and original sin. Nevertheless, gluttony is responsible for a multitude of sins, especially drunkenness.

Before the fall, God gave man dominion over nature, but because of original sin, nature has usurped man's authority. Now some people are so deeply under the authority of nature that they are slaves to it. One of the many consequences of original sin is that plants got dominion over man. The alcoholic is addicted to many plants and these plants have become his master. The plants used in beer, wine, whiskey, heroin, and cocaine are just a few. There is strawberry, blueberry, blackberry, apple, peach, grape, and rice wine. Corn, barley, and hops are in beer. Whiskey uses other plants. Jesus does not want anybody to be a slave to a substance that defiles the temple of His Holy Spirit.

Mankind has a God-given desire to eat and drink, but gluttony is an ungodly desire to lustfully consume inordinate amounts of excess food and drink. Gluttony overrides self-regulation. A compulsive, insatiable craving for these necessary items takes charge. The vice is learned, and once established, the pathological hunger drive is virtually unstoppable. The habit of indulgence dominates character, so much so that the person merits the name of the vice. They are no longer a person who overeats, they are a glutton.

Of all the foods and drinks a glutton could crave, the most sorry glutton is the one who craves alcohol. Proverbs 23:20-21 states that the drunk glutton will fall into ruin. The vice of gluttony is exponentially strengthened when alcohol is the substance consumed. To alcoholics, drinking is perceived as a need instead of a want and they become slaves to their drunken appetite. They would not share a bottle of wine with friends, but would drink three bottles alone. Gluttony that is associated with food promotes secondary sins like sloth, but the sins associated with gluttony for alcohol far exceed the sins of the overweight person. As drunkenness increases, the gluttonous appetite for alcohol becomes progressively pathological. The lust to hoggishly consume gluttonous amounts of alcohol is a spiritual disease. This type of gluttony is very unique and its practitioner merits the title drunkard. The drunkard is guilty of two sins: gluttony and drunkenness. Demons crave to turn a churchgoing Christian into a drunken pig.

### The Sin Complex of Drunks

Drunkenness is a very complicated, sinful behavior, which is often the tip of the iceberg or hub to many other sins. The demonic lust for the alcoholic's destruction does not stop at drunkenness. Demons use drunkenness like a ring in a bull's nose. They lead the drunk down many other sinful paths. The drunk commits sins that they would not otherwise commit. Once the demons get the drunk to be guilty of grave, habitual sin, it is relatively easy for them to convince the drunk to commit other grave sins. Demons try to turn an alcoholic's isolated sinful behavior into a lifestyle of sin. Sin transforms from an individual action into a habitual way of being. This turns a person who committed a sin into a sinner. The alcoholic becomes a drunk. Sin begets sin and drunks are no exception. Sins are piled on top of sins, destroying any accumulated grace or the effects of grace, and this reduces the probability of recovery. The frequency, intensity, and duration of physical craving and psychological temptation increase with each committed sin. All sin lowers the resistance to commit sin. It feeds and strengthens the spiritual disease, allowing it to further ensnare the alcoholic. Drunkenness effects all areas of life. It is not isolated. The only people who believe it is isolated are the drunks. When the milestones on the road spiraling downward are studied it is obvious that many of those behaviors which caused the drunk to hit bottom were actually sins. For example, many drunks lie about their drinking. Lying is a sin. They may be too hung over to go to church. Maybe they committed adultery while drunk. Obviously, drunken violence only occurs while drunk. The sin of drunkenness promotes a myriad of other sins. Likewise, the commission of a sin not directly related to drunkenness will lessen the alcoholic's ability to resist the sin of drunkenness. In this weakened condition the demons come in for the kill. Drunkenness is the head of the beast and must be cut off. Drunkenness is never an excuse to commit additional sin. The argument, "I did not mean to do it, but I was drunk," does not fool anyone except the drunk.

    Many of the sins associated with drunkenness are not in themselves functionally autonomous. Since these secondary sins are a function of drunkenness they will continue as long as the alcoholic continues to get drunk. Once the drunk begins recovery they can often stop the associated sin. Through resisting the temptation to drink, the alcoholic becomes more able to resist alcohol and generally becomes more able to resist all sin. The Christian alcoholic could more quickly progress in recovery if he were cautious to avoid all sin, not only sin associated with drunkenness.

## Enabling is a Sin

Enabling allows the drunk to continue in his folly, usually by removing the negative consequences of what would naturally occur. In its milder form, it allows the drunk's life to be easier.

The guilt of the drunk's sin may be incurred by another because they enable the drunk. They may think they are helping but actually they are giving the drunk refuge from justice. The enabler shares in the drunk's guilt when they partner in the sin by going to the store and buying the drunk's booze or by calling in sick for them. When someone knows that a drunk is going to drive, they share in the sin if they are silent. It is hard to prevent the belligerent drunk from driving or to call the police on a drunken spouse or friend, but murder by proxy is hard to bare. When someone brags about the drunk's behavior as if it were funny instead of the crying shame it actually is, they share in the drunk's sin and guilt. Complicity is incurred when someone defends the drunk's evil. To defend sinful behavior because the perpetrator was drunk means you concur with the sin.

## Fallen Angels: The Forgotten Variable in Drunkenness

The reason demonic involvement in drunkenness is forgotten is because demonic success is very dependent on secrecy. Alcoholics can prevent demons from having the advantage over them if they understand the demonic methods to damn (2 Corinthians 2:11). The church has authority and power over demons. Unfortunately, there is a lack of knowledge in the church regarding demonic power and Christian authority. The purpose of this section is to inform on Satan's top-secret plans. The drunk will begin to know how his enemy, the demons, manipulate him. Satan does not want the alcoholic to know that Christians can take authority over him in Jesus' name. He is very happy that Christians are usually on the defensive rather than on the offensive. He does not want them to know that he is already defeated.

**Demonic Aggression**

Demonic aggression has historically been part of the theories of personality, psychopathology, and physical illness. The vast reservoir of ancient literature is teeming with illustrations. But just because ancient or pagan religions acknowledge demonic aggression as the cause of illness is not a valid reason for Christians to accept their observations and conclusions. For Christians, the Holy Bible teaches that demonic aggression did exist and today's clergy reaffirm it. The Bible illustrates that demons afflict man in ways that modern psychologists call psychopathology and modern physicians call physical illness. Today as in ancient times, many labels describe the types of attack demons use on mankind. Each label expresses a slight difference in the victim's level of cooperation. Labels like schizophrenia, multiple personality disorder, drunkenness, and epilepsy are sometimes caused by direct demonic intervention.

Demonic aggression can come from outside the body (1 Peter 5:8, Job 1:6-19). These attacks include temptation, oppression, curses, sins of others, witchcraft, and the act of a demon trying to possess a person. Attacks also come from inside the body (Matthew 8:16). These attacks include original sin, demonic possession, generational curses, and illness. The inside/outside dichotomy does not always explain the true dynamic in the drunk. For instance, sin is committed when temptation (outside), activates the old sin nature (inside).

There are also types of demonic aggression for which a person cannot be held personally accountable. These include original sin, illness directly caused by original sin, generational curses, demons trying to take possession, some cases of demonic possession, and certain temptations. At times, the drunk who experiences demonic aggression is completely innocent. At other times, the drunk who experiences demonic aggression rightfully deserves it as a consequence to his action.

Satan is very aggressive in battle. He roams the earth as a lion seeking someone to devour (1 Peter 5:8). Satan is so sly that he can appear as an angel of light (2 Corinthians 11:14). Since he can appear as an angel of light he can take many other deceiving forms to cause the alcoholic to relapse. He would look like an ice-cold beer if that would cause a relapse.

**The Demonic Personality-Know Your Enemy**

Lucifer committed the original sin, not Adam. This original sin is recorded in Isaiah 14:13-14, not in Genesis 3:6. A multitude of sins occurred when one-third of the angels followed Satan. Adam and Eve committed the first, or original, sin in human nature. God did not spare the angels when they sinned. Some angels were cast to hell (2 Peter 2:4) and some were cast to Earth (12:7-9, Ezekiel 28:13-17, Isaiah 14:12). The rebellious angels were cast down and stripped of all their grace. Since they had to exist in their mere nature, their sin nature worsened. Their evil personalities are the opposite of God's revealed personality. God's personality can be seen in Galatians 5:22-23, "But the fruit of the Spirit is love, joy, peace, patience, kindness, goodness, faithfulness, gentleness, and self-control." The fallen angels' personality traits are none of these; in fact, the opposite describes them. The demonic personality is full of hatred, unhappiness, despair, dissension, discord, restlessness, impatience, wickedness, deceitfulness, rudeness, and vulgarity. It is inflamed, stirred-up, and crazed. Let's not forget that it is also full of sinfulness. This is the natural development of their wicked personalities existing for millenniums without healing grace. Just like fallen man, they have a multitude of psychological problems. The demonic personality sounds a lot like the drunk's personality.

For example, demons have a delusion of persecution. An argument could be made that demons are not experiencing a delusion since there are Christian spiritual warriors binding and hindering them. Nevertheless, demons are truly paranoid, even about nothing. They are liars and even lie to themselves. That is the nature of all megalomaniacs with a God complex. God blinds them from many spiritual realities. They are damned but do not believe it. Specifically, Satan is in denial about his defeat and rationalizes his great anguish and anger. He is under the delusion that it is better to rule on Earth than to serve in Heaven. He really believes that he could have sat and reigned on God's throne. His delusions keep him content.

When God created Adam and anointed him sovereign over all the Earth, Satan's pain became aggravated. Satan knew he had to break Adam's fellowship with the Holy Spirit, the walks with Jesus in the Garden, and the blessings of God the Father. He knew that if Adam were allowed to continue in fellowship with God, Adam would eventually bind him and his kingdom. Satan made battle plans. Part of the plan was to attack Adam without declaring war. Satan never said, "I am Satan, a damned angel with plans to damn you. Listen to my instruction," even though this was his true intention. Satan remembered that God did not forgive him. So he did to Adam just what he did to one-third of the angels: He lied to him and bore false witness against God. Satan convinced Adam that he could literally become a god himself instead of merely being in God's image and likeness. He presented Adam with the means to accomplish that desire. Adam accepted Satan's will and disobeyed God. It was the true world war, because the world was the prize. A war fought and won in a single battle, which changed the natural course of human development.

Satan and man received a common punishment: both became fallen creatures, but God had more mercy on mankind. He promised mankind a Redeemer. The difference in punishment absolutely confounded and enraged Satan.

Satan and his demons contrive situations for our eternal damnation. Compared to man, demons are dangerously intelligent. Their sheer age has allowed them to acquire virtually limitless knowledge on how to damn us. To damn us, the demonic behaviors are legion, but in summary they try to defile us, to deceive us, to torment us, to enslave us, to compel us, to possess us, and to kill us. This can all be accomplished through drunkenness.

Jesus is the Head of His body, and Satan is the head of his body. As Jesus has different parts of His body with different functions, ministries and gifts, Satan has different parts of his body, with different functions, ministries, and gifts. The mind of Christ and the mind of Satan both desire to recreate themselves in the mind of man. God energizes the soul, makes it more perfect, holy, and in the image of Christ's. Satan also energizes the soul, but to diabolical ends.

### Direct Demonic Influence

Demons are expert psychologists. They can begin work on a normal healthy person and within a very short time transform them into an emotionally disturbed, nasty, irresponsible drunk. The demonic power to create emotional havoc is greatly increased in the alcoholic. The drunk's sin nature is so powerful that he is more in the image of the demon's than God's. The reason demons have more control over the drunk is because they approach man through the old nature, which is very alive and active. Drunkenness starves the soul and strategically attacks that part of the personality that resists sin. Each time alcoholics drink they are actually feeding, nourishing, and empowering the demons. Everyone knows that alcohol reduces inhibitions. The drunk becomes progressively more susceptible to demons. This demonstrates the demons' ability to cause the progression of alcoholism. Drunks are not the masters of their own wills. Demons manipulate the drunk toward the road to hell as a puppeteer controls a puppet.

Traditionally there are nine orders of angels. The proper title for many of these different orders is obscured by the different translations of the Bible, but Webster's New Collegiate Dictionary, starting with the lowest rank, classifies them as: angels, archangels, principalities, powers, virtues, dominions, thrones, cherubim, and seraphim. There is biblical evidence of a hierarchy within the angelic choirs. Matthew 12:45 shows that a demon cast out of a person will return with seven more wicked demons. In order for the seven new demons to be more wicked there must be a ranking in terms of wickedness and power. Another example occurred when the apostles were sent by Jesus to minister. Some returned saying that they could not cast out a demon from a boy. In Mark 9:29, Jesus said, "....this kind can come out only by prayer." When Jesus said "this kind," He implicitly declared that there are "other kinds," which are easier to cast out. Jesus made a distinction between the power of certain demons to bond more strongly.

There is a difference between demons in terms of rank. Lucifer was a cherub (Ezekiel 28:13-16). St. Paul writes about powers, principalities, and dominations. One of the major deceptions Satan has placed in the minds of most Christians is that there is no difference between him and the other demons. Many Christians interchange the words Satan, devil, and demons as if they were synonymous. Demons or devils are words used to describe all the other fallen angels, the powers, principalities, and thrones, but not the cherub Satan. Satan tormented Adam, Job, and Jesus, not demons. Demons possessed Mary Magdalene and the man at Gennesaret. Generally, demons attack alcoholics, not Satan.

**Temptation**

Some people experience strong temptation for short intervals, others constantly experience weak temptation. Some people live years without much temptation while others are constantly being attacked. Although the degree and frequency of temptation varies, its continued presence is part of man's fallen nature. Everyone on Earth experiences temptation. When temptation is constant and overwhelming, it is usually demonically inspired, not natural mortal flesh expressing its depraved nature.

Temptation is especially hard to keep out of the mind since it can erupt into consciousness with or without stimuli. The alcoholic does not recognize temptation as coming from an external demonic source. They perceive the temptation as springing up from within themselves. If alcoholics correctly perceived the temptation to drink as a type of telepathy from demons, many would reject the thought. The demonic strategy is to trick alcoholics into believing that drinking is their own idea.

Demons are flexible in the type of temptation they propose to the alcoholic. Demons know that some recovering alcoholics are better equipped to resist psychological temptation so they cause biological craving for alcohol. Sometimes the easy way to get a sober alcoholic to drink is simply non-specific physical stress or anxiety. They simply want to damn a soul to hell. Demons are damned, not stupid. They perceive the weakest link and mercilessly attack.

### Generational Curses

A curse occurs when God or demons inflict injury. Proclaiming a curse is not always a sin, since God's prophets have pronounced curses, and God Himself has sent curses. All curses through witchcraft are always a sin. There is rarely a Christian justification for pronouncing a curse because Jesus instructed Christians to love their enemies and bless those who curse them. A generational curse is the opposite of a generational blessing.

Many cultures have believed that the sins of the parents are passed down to the children. There is scriptural evidence to support this. In Exodus 20:5, 34:7; Numbers 14:18; and Deuteronomy 5:9-10; God stated that He will adversely affect the third and fourth generations of a sinner even though the sinner's descendants are innocent. When one complains that they should not have to suffer the consequences of someone else's sin, they would do well to recall that they pray to the Father through the benefits of Christ even though they were not personally crucified.

When demons attach themselves to a family line for consecutive generations their demonic character is superimposed on each successive generation. This gives the appearance that there is a common family trait passed on, but it is a common demon that is passed on. The demons become integrated into the family's collective personality; therefore the human counterpart of the unholy union does not recognize a demon. Generational curses spread evil, not only by the addition of people but also through time, sometimes for centuries. In the case of Adam's sin, for all time.

Initially, one person is the very first in a family's history to be the recipient of a curse. They either committed a sin which called down God's judgment or else they were the innocent victim of someone who pronounced an incantation for harm to befall them. Regardless of the victim's culpability, they become the special project of demons. This is only a personal curse. It becomes a generational curse when it is transferred to descendants. When the fourth generation commits the sins caused by the curse, they become the ascendant who passes the curse to the third and fourth generations.

The parents, grandparents, or great grandparents could establish the curse. That adds up to 14 ascendants that could initiate a generational curse. Sometimes grandparents or parents call evil upon their grandchildren or children. For some reason, curses directed to a descendent bond more strongly. When an ascendant says, "God damn you!" or "Go to hell," they have just invoked a curse. These are curses, not mere profanity. Once they cool down they regret the curse, but in the heat of the night, they meant what they said. Sometimes people in anger curse someone but only halfheartedly. This is not a grave sin. It is a small sin.

Drunkenness itself has the power to bring down God's curse upon the drunk. They deserve any curse. Unfortunately, many of the worst drunks and dry drunks have a generational curse for which they are innocent victims. Much illness is transmitted by demons through generational curses.

Just because an evil person invokes a curse does not mean that it will stick to its intended victim. God alone controls the level and degree of demonic aggression. If the intended victim were especially holy, a curse would not take. Curses, even terrible curses pronounced by a powerful occultist, will be powerless to the degree of its intended victim's holiness. A very holy person is virtually immune to a curse, but the more evil a person, the more power over them a curse has. The drunk not only has no protection from the curses of man, but actually draws down God's curse. Unfortunately for the drunk, they cannot make the claim of being especially holy. Therefore, if a curse is pronounced they have little protection.

Illness is passed down through biological, psychological, and spiritual causes. There are illnesses that are attributed to generational curses but are not supernatural. Sometimes nature, through genetics or psychology, passes dispositions or physical illnesses to successive generations. There are two types of generational curses-supernatural and natural.

## Supernatural Generational Curses

In Deuteronomy 7:25-26, God forbids the possession of occult objects. While the owner of occult objects becomes cursed like the object, the child brought up in a house that contains occult objects is especially at risk of becoming generationally cursed. In addition, any parental involvement with the occult such as witchcraft, seances, astrology, tarot, parapsychology, etc., increases the likelihood of the supernatural transfer of a generational curse.

There was an event that gave the demons a legal right to implement and pass on the curse. A supernatural generational curse does not necessarily mean that a demon takes possession of family members. Often it's a lesser form of aggression.

Demons move in and out of families with generational curses according to their own demonic agenda. Sometimes the supernatural generational curse skips a generation or sibling.

## Natural Generational Curses

While supernatural generational curses are caused by direct demonic aggression, natural generational curses are caused by observation and learning. If the parents are not careful they may transfer learned sinful behavior to their children. After all, the child was born and raised by sinners, and is personally a sinner.

Sins of the parents can be transferred to the next generation through physical, psychological, or spiritual deprivation. Children deprived of these stimuli find it very difficult as adults to comfortably interact with other adults. When a young child is deprived of spiritual stimuli, spiritual damage occurs. For example, when atheists deprive their children of Godly spiritual stimuli, the child's soul becomes qualitatively different from the child brought up in a Christian home. The spiritual predisposition that comes from a Christian upbringing is lacking. Spiritually deprived children are also more susceptible to the transfer of a supernatural generational curse.

Generational curses can also be transferred by pathogenic family patterns or abuse. Some families are more than severely dysfunctional. The degree of psychopathology is so intense that even the outside observer feels weird by association. The family generates a dysfunctional synergy that appears far beyond that of mortal man. Nevertheless, it is not spiritual. It is very normal for children of drunks to become drunks. The behaviors of today set things in motion, which affect later generations.

## Why Demons Possess

Demonic possession does not cause alcoholism, but man's sin nature and external prodding by demons (temptation) causes it. Drunkenness is a sin like any other grave sin. There is no demon living inside the alcoholic person that can be expelled to cause sobriety. Nevertheless, many alcoholics become possessed while drunk. In the olden days, alcohol was called spirits because everybody knew that drunks became possessed. Hard liquor is called spirits for this very reason. Demons like to get drunk, but cannot do it until they possess. They really like its altered state and often enter any drunken person they observe. The demonic rage demonstrated by drunks correlated with blackouts is clinical evidence of demonic possession. How could a parent or spouse reap such hell on their loved ones? They could not, but demons could!

We know demons desire to be equal to or greater than God, since that was why they were cast from Heaven. They have possession confused with worship since possession by God's Holy Spirit is worship. Demons would do anything to receive God's glory. The irony is that they believe they naturally and rightly deserve that glory even though they receive it only by deception. When demons receive worship from man they get a perverted sense of self worth. That is one reason why praise and worship of God is so powerful: demons are being rejected. Holy worship emotionally hurts demons. Their pathology compels them to possess. Demons possess people to keep them away from God. They fear the potential of a drunk who may be converted and then battle against them. They perceive possession as a sign of their power over the drunk. They possess so that in eternity their humans would outnumber God's. Satan got 33 percent of the angels but fights to get as close to 100 percent of the humans as possible. Possession occurs because that is the only way demons can directly impact the world. They materialize through the host body into the physical realm. In the host body they have the ability to speak (Mark 1:24). They can express their knowledge (Acts 19:15). In addition to expressing their mind, they can express their will (Matthew 12:44, Mark 5:12). Fallen angels who possess are actually parasites living off the human body. In this sense, a demon that possesses a human can be compared to a maggot, louse, tapeworm, mosquito, or other parasite. They are the worst type of parasite a human can have because many ministers cannot discern their presence, and to the scientific healer they do not exist.

# THE PROGRESSION OF THE SPIRITUAL DISEASE

The human body is a marvelous creation of God. Humans are physical, psychological, and spiritual creatures. Any one of these three component systems can become diseased and transfer the disease into the other. This means that anything that happens in one component system (spirit, mind, or body) causes stimulus and response phenomena, and feedback loops in the other components. To explain the disease of alcoholism on any individual component level is insufficient and not descriptive of the true process. There is constant conversion and transformation between the three component systems; therefore, the disease of alcoholism can never be isolated in any single component system. The whole affects each component, while each component affects the whole. The disease freely moves throughout the triune nature of man in parallel. When the spirit is diseased, the mind and body reflect that damage because they serve as the spirits barometer and indicate its condition. Physical and psychological processes occur virtually simultaneously and are different aspects of the very same disease process. When a spiritual disease transforms, it converts into a psychological and/or biological disorder. The supernatural and natural diseases are inseparably bound up with each other in the same way as flesh and blood or spirit and soul.

As God is triune, composed of Father, Son, and Holy Spirit, man is triune, composed of spirit, soul, and body. Man in God's image is a unitary creation divided into three separate components. The human soul is itself triune in nature, composed of three separate but interacting aspects. They are the mind, the will, and the emotions. The mind, will, and emotions are as distinct from each other as is the Father, Son, and Holy Spirit. One God, three Persons. One soul, three functional aspects. No component of man's triune nature acts independent of the other components. Instead they act in tandem.

## How Progression Takes Place

The progression of the disease begins with experimentation, then proceeds through abuse, habit formation, increased tolerance, dependence, psychopathology and spiritual destruction. The amount of alcohol consumed increases and it damages body systems. During this process, there are increased social, behavioral, and spiritual problems. As the disease progresses, family, employment, money, emotional, medical, legal, etc., problems also increase.

Long term alcohol use causes the body to adapt so that its absence creates a disruption in the body's function, even at the cellular level. Therefore, a standard dose does not create the same desirable effect. In order to achieve this same effect a larger quantity needs to be drunk and the alcoholic is only too happy to oblige. Years earlier when he was experimenting with alcohol, six beers would get him drunk. As tolerance increased, he often needed six beers to feel normal. Any person who drinks enough will develop tolerance and become physically dependent.

As the disease progresses it eventually damages various body systems. Demons know that the mind, will, and emotions can be directly influenced through the brain. So the author of illness often attacks the physical brain. Chronic drunkenness not only initiates permanent brain damage; its effects carry over even when sober. When the effects of alcohol damage the brain, drunken behavior becomes even more bizarre. This makes the demons especially happy because they not only have victory over the soul but have also advanced their battle line to the realm of the body.

It appears that the soul is seated in the brain because a brain tumor or chemical imbalance can cause major alterations in the soul's mind, will, or emotions. When a man dies the brain is dead but the mind, will, and emotions still exist. Therefore, the soul's existence is not dependent on the brain's existence, but its function is. The brain merely stores memories. Nerve impulses achieve psychological representation within the spiritual realm, not the brain. The brain is the interface for body and soul.

The drunk's interaction with other fallen souls, combined with the wear and tear of daily life can itself cause sickness. Even when the person is a Christian, daily wear has its bad effects. Imagine what it is like for a drunk who is not renewed by God's grace.

Psychological dependence is different than biological dependence because it is not based on the drug's action on the body. When a person, place, thing, or event is repeatedly paired with drunkenness, these become a stimulus to cause drunkenness. For example, if the alcoholic gets drunk in a bar, then that environment becomes empowered to elicit drunken behavior. It establishes a matrix between the alcoholic and his environment, which reinforces drunkenness. It is more powerful than physical dependence because it takes longer to become free from than physical dependence.

When the ability to drink becomes thwarted, the desire becomes more intense. The desire to drink becomes so impelling that the alcoholic loses sight of its bad effects. If the alcoholic does not drink, an unbearable tension builds up. Its release comes only by drinking. Ironically, the drunkenness so desperately craved to quench the burning desire for alcohol only increases the intensity of the burning desire. The more the drunk drinks, the more insatiable his desire becomes and the less it satisfies. The appetite for alcohol is increased rather than satisfied.

There are two opposing processes that cannot operate simultaneously in the sober alcoholic. The first is the forward momentum of grace. To the degree this process is in operation the second process, the progression of the disease, is hindered. Note hindered, not eradicated. The progression of the disease is always just below the surface, ready to spring up, with repressed or suppressed force. As soon as the forward momentum of grace ceases, the progression of the disease rears its ugly head and tries to make up for the time lost when grace was dominant.

There was a time when a person drank to help relieve some problems, but over time the disease progressed to become an autonomous problem with its own life. For example, instead of being a symptom of a bad marriage, it transformed into a monster and became one of the reasons for the bad marriage. As the disease progresses the drunk transforms from being a happy drunk and often becomes more violent. When alcohol changes from being the drunk's friend and comforter into an enemy and persecutor, progression has reached a new milestone. The psychopathology of alcoholism is well established when the drunk begins to drink to control the symptoms of withdrawal.

Progression becomes evident when the drunk will drink anything that has alcohol in it. They may be beer drinkers and actually hate the taste of whiskey, but at 3 a.m. when they finished their 24th beer, whiskey or even vanilla extract is attractive to the psychotically drunk.

The only light that guides the drunk's footsteps is the light emitted from hell's fires. It is a terrible light to be led by, especially when Jesus is the light of the world and the drunk could amend his ways and bask in holy light.

## Formation of Vice

Habit formation is the primary mechanism that converts spiritual disorders into psychological or biological illness. The mechanism itself is spiritually neutral but can attach itself to either virtue or vice. Demons hate good habits in humans and try to encourage the development of bad habits, like drunkenness.

One of the causes of drunkenness is the development of a bad habit. The human ability to learn is a mechanism demons use to advance their kingdom. Behaviors become easier to accomplish each time they are repeated. Habit makes drinking automatic; it becomes second nature. They are called second nature because they appear as natural as an instinct. Now the desire to drink changes, giving it previously unimaginable power. The person no longer plans to drink, instead they naturally find themselves drinking. Habit removes a behavior from being a conscious willful act and transforms it into a reflexive instinctive act. They consistently drink without thinking. The decision-making process is bypassed each time the same situation arises. Habits partially explain why some people sin and others do not when exposed to the same temptation.

Since demons are not omnipresent, economy of effort is important and habit formation takes the pressure off them. Through habit formation demons have the alcoholic automatically doing their diabolical will. Habit formation allows demons to take a less aggressive stance against the drunk because it places them on automatic pilot and steers them in the direction of hell. Demons do not have to tempt the drunk to drink because they automatically drink. That is why demons particularly like the tool of alcohol to damn a soul to hell. The road to hell through drunkenness requires less demonic effort than any other method. This frees up the demons to apply their evil craft elsewhere and roam the earth looking to devour more souls. They use only the most efficient means to damn a soul.

They try to turn a person's isolated sinful behavior into a lifestyle of sin. If a person had one sexual drunken experience, the demons try to lessen the soul's perception of wrongdoing and increase the body's perception of pleasure so that the sin is repeated.

## Alcoholics Learn To Be Helpless

The downward spiral to hell experienced by all drunks is a vicious circle of learned helplessness and hopelessness. No matter how often they try to begin recovery, they fail. It does not matter if they begged God to heal them, made a vow to God that they would abstain, or promised their spouse. They either cannot initiate or maintain recovery. They really think their efforts are useless and a waste of time. They give up trying. They have learned to be helpless. To illustrate, at the circus, large elephants are restrained by little chains and a small stake in the ground. The elephant has the power to effortlessly break free but does not. It has learned to be helpless. This is accomplished by fastening a huge chain to a baby elephant's leg and the other end to a huge tree. Like a wild stallion being broken, the baby elephant violently tries to break free but cannot. The chain and tree are much too strong. Eventually the elephant learns that pulling is useless and stops. The trainer progressively uses lighter chains and replaces the tree with a small stake. The elephant does not ever pull hard enough to break free because it has learned to be helpless. Just as animal trainers teach the elephants to be helpless, demons train the drunks.

Another example occurs when a child grows up and repeatedly hears that he is stupid. The term self-fulfilling prophecy describes a phenomena in which the probability of an event occurring increases simply because someone expects it to happen. Negative reinforcement from parents and teachers actually program the child for failure. The child perceives learning as unpleasant and has no interest in understanding new ideas or concepts. Developmental and academic challenges are unusually stressful and feared. He becomes very critical of his own mistakes and does not realize others make similar mistakes. After years of thinking this way the child actually is less intelligent.

Often the label of alcoholic or drunk prevents recovery or causes relapse. The world view develops to accommodate the label. Even the alcoholic's family begins to treat him differently because of the label. They may let him get away with behaviors that would otherwise not be tolerated. Through learned helplessness the alcoholic accepts the lifestyle of the label. His motivation for health is destroyed by unconscious morbidity. The label become a self-fulfilling prophecy.

Many assume that the drunk just does not care. Actually they have experienced so many negative consequences that they have come to expect them. They feel that it's useless to try so why bother, they are just going to fail. The drunks who have learned to be helpless have great difficulty in recovery because they are retarded in their ability to learn how to act as a sober person.

## Alcoholics Become Defensive

Although there are healthy defenses like the innate aversion to sin, there are also the defensive reactions, which are defects. Everyone unconsciously uses psychological defense mechanisms. Alcoholics use them but to a pathological degree. If they did not rely on them their anxiety level would probably cause a heart attack. When used in excess, the internal resources that generate them can become depleted. Sometimes they are re-energized continuously but at other times the infrastructure collapses. Coping with stress fails when a person cannot master the stressful event. They can either use defensive thoughts like denial or they can use defense-oriented behaviors like drunkenness.

Drunkenness, like all addictions, keeps its victim from experiencing reality. Drunks are not usually consciously aware of the stress they are being bombarded with, but it is building up in their subconscious. In order to avoid the painful consequences of drunkenness the alcoholic recreates reality by lies, cover-ups, projection, and other devices. The drunk drinks deeply from the cups of delusion and denial. When drunks continue to explain away their bad behavior, a subconscious discomfort builds up and they progressively become stressed out. The addicted personality prevents them from perceiving that drunkenness has caused spiritual death.

The sick soul develops a defensive structure, which is supported by the sick soul's misperceived reality and functions to protect its own self-existence. For example, a woman married to an abusive, drunken husband may not recognize his behavior as abusive because everyone tells her that her husband is a good man or because she subconsciously believes she deserves it. The subconscious is a very powerful controlling force in the human psyche. It controls a lot of behavior, sinful or not. Much thinking takes place in the subconscious concurrent with conscious thoughts, feelings, and volition. The drunk's subconscious is more messed up than his conscience. This should not detract from the fact that his conscience is very depraved. His use of defense mechanisms is extensive.

Drunkenness, if started early in life, retards the development of the mind, will, and emotions. So, the adult drunk may be 75 chronological years old but key functions are operating on a much younger level. The alcoholic's character took many years to develop and it gets worse each day. As drunkenness continues, pathology becomes superimposed on the retarded functions. Drunkenness causes the formation of an addicted personality, which competes with the natural personality until it wins. With the establishment of the addicted personality the drunk begins to act more and more bizarre.

Some unfortunate drunks are not merely mean and nasty, but psychotic. They experience a pathological intoxication when drinking. They have progressed so deeply into the disease that even short-term abstinence causes hallucinations. Others experience blackouts at a frequency that would scare most people sober.

## Destruction of the Conscience

Conscience is possibly the highest, most noble aspect, the crowning glory that sets man most in the image and likeness of God. The conscience is one of the most direct ways God communicates His will to Christians as well as non-Christians. Through the conscience, God imprints His moral law into the makeup of each individual. It is the voice of God that sounds an alarm when considering a bad thought or action. The level at which the infused conscience resides only permits script writing by God. Parental and societal values are not internalized to the same core level as God's. This acquired shaping either reinforces or destroys the God-infused conscience. While God's will is the objective standard of right and wrong, the acquired conscience is the subjective standard of right and wrong. The development of conscience is not dependent on intelligence, as uneducated dolts often know right from wrong better than the scholar does. Operationally, the infused conscience and the acquired conscience function simultaneously.

If an intended action is morally wrong the antecedent conscience is activated. It warns that the impending action is morally bankrupt. This does not happen when an impending action is morally correct. It is only activated in response to morally corrupt plans. If a person chooses to ignore the pangs of conscience and commits the action, the consequent conscience will be activated. They will experience guilt or shame. Reprobates ignore the antecedent conscience, commit the morally wrong act, and repress the shame and guilt generated by the consequent conscience. The manifestation of a bad or guilty conscience did not enter the stream of time until Adam sinned.

When a healthy person does something wrong, they experience guilt. A healthy conscience guides and accuses. The drunk's conscience mostly accuses and they resist its guidance, therefore the drunk reaps what he sows. Drunkenness is objectively and intrinsically wrong whether the conscience approves or disapproves.

When drunks fall under the delusion that their sinful behavior is justified, they have rejected their conscience and become reprobates. Under strong delusion and blindness of mind they call their vice a virtue. They are proud of their drinking ability. Doing wrong and thinking it is right is itself evidence of the disease's progression.

At one time the alcoholic's conscience convicted him and he realized that his drunken behavior was a sin. Committing sin desensitizes the conscience to sin's repugnance and increases the probability of committing the next sin. Instead of using the pain of conscience as a catalyst to repent, they continued to sin and were handed over to the demons. Drunks harden their consciences and lose interest in repentance.

The degree which people perceive their conscience varies tremendously. Some are very sensitive, while others are pathologically insensitive. Reprobates may appear to have deadened their conscience, but they can never completely destroy it. Despite the drunk's desire to silence the voice of good conscience, it persists. No matter how hard drunks try to deny their conscience, they cannot. At best they can only desensitize their mind from the conscience's good counsel. They deny the guilt of their behavior, they drown it out by drink, and they rationalize away their bad feelings. The harmful effects of guilt do not automatically go away. Their actions still cause guilt but it becomes subliminal. Repressed guilt promotes relapse, not recovery. Until the proper Christian response to guilt is administered it migrates from the conscious to the unconscious and festers, sickening the mind, will, and emotions.

    Drunks have been handed over to the demons because of their hardness of heart and only God's mercy can release them from the depraved state they find themselves in. The deadening of conscience is also responsible for destroying faith (1 Tim 1:18-19). This is the main reason drunks become atheists. A guilty conscience causes the alcoholic to avoid God. The alcoholic in recovery needs to be able to freely approach God.

    The priests who Jesus talked about performed church services, circumcisions, and sacrifices, but inwardly they were of the devil, not God. There was an obvious inconsistency between what these people practiced and what they preached. Hypocrisy among the clergy is ancient. The phenomenon that clergy with ministries get God's anointing for the purpose of that specific ministry is not new. The phenomenon that some clergy with ministries go to hell is also not new. God teaches that on Judgement Day some will be sentenced to the second death (Revelation 20:12-15). At the Judgement some that are sentenced to the second death will be surprised because during their life they had a powerful ministry. Knowing this, how can anyone presume they are going to heaven? If these powerful ministers of healing are under delusion, what then of the Christians without powerful ministries who assume they are going to heaven? What then of the drunk? What will it take to convict the heart of the drunken reprobate? Will they have to stand before God's throne and hear Him say, "Go away unfaithful servant, I never knew you?" Translated, this means he was an unrepentant sinner. His unholy, drunken life merits hell. Therefore, he goes to hell.

Many drunks falsely believe that they are going to heaven. Reprobates living in sin will inherit the second death, not the kingdom of God. These drunks have self righteously stood in God's place and judged their eternal station. This is very presumptuous. This delusion delights demons.

## Alcohol Induced Disorders of the Will

While paranoia is a disorder of the mind and affective psychoses are disorders of the emotions, will disorders are more elusive. The will has a pathology unique to its nature. This pathology manifests itself as the inability to perceive God's will, opposition to God's will, the inability to accomplish God's will, and confusing God's will with either the demonic will or with self will. It also manifests itself as willpower weakness. These are mankind's primary volitional disorders. These disorders are exponentially amplified when applied to the drunk.

Man's will is a more precious target for Satan than his mind, emotions, or body. To directly control the will, he would gladly loosen his hold on many minds, emotions, and bodies. The will is spiritual. That is how demons short-circuit the will; they use spiritual powers.

## Inability to Perceive God's Will

It is often difficult, virtually impossible, or the exceptional case when even the mature Christian can correctly perceive God's will for all the details of their life. This is because it is God's will that His will is not completely known. He sovereignly elects not to disclose such information.

Many want to know God's will about their lives when in fact they are not doing God's known will in the present. If they are not trustful in small things, how do they reason to merit knowing more? God often reveals only that which is immediately necessary. If they are not doing God's known will why are they frustrated when they do not know what grand plans, if any, He has in store for them? How can the recently sober alcoholic lay claim to knowing God's will for his life? His ability to correctly perceive God's will is greatly damaged because of the progression of the disease. What claim on knowing God's will can the drunk have when he is living in very grave sin? To the drunk, God's call is simple. Stop drinking!

## Opposition to God's Will

God's will constitutes the objective moral order, not man's. Ideally, God's will should be the driving force behind human action. Certainly not the pathological will of the alcoholic in early recovery, or the drunk. It is God's will that everybody, including the alcoholic, do His will, but the drunk opposes God's will by living in the sin of drunkenness. God wants the drunk to repent and do good things in accordance with His will. When the focus of the recovering alcoholic's will is God's will, the pressures of relapse wear little on the personality. When either Satan, self, the world, or the spirit of the world are the will's focus, instability and error reign. The probability of relapse also increases.

## Inability to Accomplish God's Will

The alcoholic paradox is this: as the will becomes powerless to resist the temptation, the compulsion itself actually increases in intensity. Resistance only increases the abnormal desire for alcohol. As the disease progresses, the will becomes so weakened, depraved, corrupt, and powerless that resistance to the compulsion to drink is virtually futile. The part of the will that helps the drunk get his next drink actually becomes strengthened. This process of resistance transforming into pathological desire is the disease of alcoholism made manifest. There is a milestone on the road to hell where drinking becomes out of control, and the drunken alcoholic has long since passed that point. Satan will do anything he can to distract a person from doing God's will. He places competing thoughts, procrastination, etc., in the alcoholic's mind as easily as we breathe.

Sometimes a person wants to do something but cannot, or else they do something they do not want to do. Both of these situations demonstrate that the will can be temporarily overridden. "The spirit is willing but the flesh is weak," demonstrates that the body's desires can sometimes override the will's intention. The will's intention remains firm, but its ability to accomplish its goal is blocked. Many drunks want to be sober but cannot muster what is needed because their flesh is weak and warring against their spirit. When a person feels compelled to sin but intellectually does not want to commit the sin, subconscious urges and cravings are in motion. These subconscious thoughts are "stinking thinking," and convert into relapse.

## Confusing God's Will With The Demonic Will and Self Will

There is usually a great difference between a person's will, the devil's will, and God's will. Man often has a plan of his own and projects that plan onto God. They imagine God's will and then accept it as valid by misdirected faith. They follow their own desire while believing God is leading them. The recently sober alcoholic cannot correctly perceive the difference between demonic or holy prompting. Yet they claim to know God's will for them!

The drunk is often led by his own will because he possesses the ability to think and act for himself. When an alcoholic follows his own desires, goals, and plans he is usually wrongly motivated.

### Willpower Weakness

Many people think that the drunk is weak willed. The point to remember about drunks is that they are not weak willed. When confronted with obstacles that hinder their consumption of alcohol, they demonstrate much willpower. They can always get alcohol no matter how adverse the conditions to acquire it.

Eventually it does not take willpower to initiate drinking, but it takes willpower to stop drinking. Their will has been so damaged that willpower only exists to do whatever is necessary to drink. The disease progresses to the point where the alcoholic not only loses the desire to become sober but also the willpower. This is especially true with the advanced, chronic drunk.

Their willpower is not applied to recovery because of lack of interest, intention, or willingness. This means that sobriety does not usually have a high priority on the drunk's list of things to do. The drunk is doing as he wills without regard to God's will or sanity. Drunkenness is more pleasing to them than sobriety. They cannot initiate sobriety by an act of will because the core intent of their will is corrupt and wrongly disposed. They really want to continue drinking, and any spark toward sobriety fails to ignite willpower. So the problem is not willpower but rather what the desires of their will are.

Some wish they were sober, but there is a big difference between wishing to be sober and to be willing to experience the painful trek of sobriety. When the drunk merely wishes to be sober they cannot muster the willpower to execute the act. The drunk's wish has no impact on movement toward the goal of sobriety. They may truly wish not to drink, but they still do. They cannot summon the internal willpower to carry out their good intentions. Remember, the road to hell is paved with good intentions.

There is value in noble resolutions, even when not actually carried out, because they provide direction for progress. Some drunks are always making worthless resolutions to stop drinking. They are usually gulping their last drink for the night when they say to themselves that this one is going to be their last drink. Instead they find themselves drinking the very next day. The wish is necessary because without it, the drunk could never begin recovery, but it is insufficient to initiate sobriety. It is merely an antecedent state to a movement of the willpower. The drunk's wish is only a thought, not the action necessary to accomplish it. A firm resolution in the form of a decision is necessary to engage the willpower. The decision initiates not only direction but also movement. The decision connects the wish for sobriety to the act of sobriety in a chain of events, which redirect and empower the will to be a causal agent in change. A drunk on the shore of a mighty river may wish he could get to the bar on the other side. His alcoholism motivates him; his body aches for a drink, but the wish for a drink and the motivation to cross the river are insufficient. The drunk needs a bridge or a boat in order to get to the other side.

Some argue that only God has true free will, but God, in His free will, decided to make man in His image and likeness. God made mankind with free will, not robots with rigid programmed responses. Human free will is divine in nature, sets mankind apart from all animals, and puts him in among the class of angels. God does not remove the freedom He granted mankind and He does not permit either the demons nor circumstance to negate that freedom. He made man self determining despite man's freedom to reject Him.

Since the fall of man, mankind's free will has become restricted. Man lost the ability to access every alternative. The drunk's freedom is restricted to a pathological degree. The drunk always has freedom of will to begin recovery but never absolute, complete, one-hundred-percent freedom. Likewise, the compulsion to drink does not possess absolute, complete, one-hundred-percent determinism. All human action is caused by a constantly fluxing ratio between freedom and determinism. It oscillates from moment to moment as well as through the course of a lifetime. Alcoholics become less free and more determined the longer they are drunks. The disease hinders the will's higher functions and it concedes to the diseased appetites of body and mind. The alcoholic suffers under a spiritual tyranny, a compulsion that is so oppressive that it appears that the ability to remain sober is beyond his free will.

In addition to the dark dungeons of the drunken nature, there are external people, places, and things that restrict the will's freedom. The human will can lose the ability to freely choose from the number of alternative options because of incomplete knowledge, a logic error, fear, psychopathology, genetics, instincts, addiction, and a myriad of other examples.

Systematic shaping by demons limits the freedom of will. Even prior decisions restrict the degrees of freedom when making any subsequent decisions. All these factors influence the will, but they do not determine its course of action. Alcoholics never objectively lose their free will, they cowardly abdicate it.

Drunks can determine reasons that they should refrain from drinking. For many alcoholics, abstinence has the same degree of freedom as holding their breath. They can hold their breath by an act of willpower, but only for a short duration. Likewise, the drunk is unable to abstain for a long duration. Extreme circumstances can supersede and override even the desire to drink. There are events and situations that can cause the worst drunk to temporarily stop drinking. This could occur because they must appear before a judge for a drunk driving citation. When the drunk is forced to abstain, his free will still chooses to drink but is obstructed. Under duress, the alcoholic would be very uncomfortable and drink as soon as possible. At the disease's final stage the drunk does not even have the ability to regulate when he will drink. Eventually, the downward spiral will accelerate and cause the drunk to be completely unable to refrain, regardless of the circumstances. This is because the law of sin is operating against the law of the spirit.

The non-alcoholic might protest that there is no good reason for the alcoholic to drink, but the drunk's compulsion is so intense that they truly perceive no alternative. They are virtually reduced to the animal level, acting on instinct and drives more than reason. What chance does the unregenerated, worldly alcoholic have in this deadly spiritual warfare? Their tunnel vision is pathological but, after all, it is a disease.

No matter how bad drunks perceive continued drunkenness, they consistently choose to drink. But this is nothing new since man has the power to do either good or evil. Through their drunken fog and diseased personality, sobriety makes sense. This is only because it is common sense and only this type of truth can get through to them.

The alcoholic does have the freedom to choose to abstain despite the raging torrent of withdrawal symptoms and desire to gratify pleasurable sensations. It's just that the odds are so stacked against them that it is extremely difficult to stop drinking. Even though they experience an overwhelming tidal wave of determinants to drink and appear predestined to die as a drunk, some can initiate recovery. They have the ability to transcend all the determinants because they are made in the image and likeness of God. This empowers them to rise from the ashes.

## Psychosomatic Manifestations

Within the Christian context, psychosomatic disorders are very real. There is a clear relationship between a person's behavior and his physical and mental condition. Proverbs 13:12, 14:30, and 17:22 confirm this link.

Psychosomatic disorders are physical ailments that are caused by psychological problems. Psychological problems are as responsible as germs, toxins, etc. Have you ever seen anyone so mad that they get a headache? Emotions change hormone and neurotransmitter production so body chemistry is changed. These changes have been known to cause physical illness.

There are several well-established correlations that illustrate the transformation pathways from the psychological to the physiological. For example, anxiety causes shortness of breath; stress causes heart attack. Anxiety and stress are examples of an emotional state already having transformed into a rudimentary physical condition. Whether conscious or unconscious, anger ferments like yeast and negatively affects the rest of the body. Anger could transform into a physical ailment like an ulcer or high blood pressure. A curse could trigger psychosomatic mechanisms through the power of suggestion. This can lead to physiological problems such as increased heart rate, respiratory distress, rashes, or high blood pressure.

The psychosomatic experts have demonstrated that certain personality types increase the probability of getting certain diseases. They say that a stressed out person is more likely to get a heart attack while an anxious person is more likely to get asthma. Generally they say that character and personality correlate with the types of illness a person would get. Since this correlation is true, what physical illness is the chronic drunk prone to since his addicted personality is relatively depraved? A really sick personality must correlate with unusually morbid physical illnesses.

There are heavenly bodies and earthly bodies (1 Corinthians 15:40). At death the natural body rises as a spiritual body (1 Corinthians 15:44). The physical body is temporal; the spiritual body is eternal. Christians should not fear what could destroy their physical bodies, but they should fear what could destroy their souls. Drunkenness destroys the body and soul.

## Alcoholics With Psychiatric Disorders

Dual diagnosis means that a person has two distinct and separate disorders, which are very interrelated. Dual diagnosis does not mean that a person is addicted to alcohol and another drug. That would be called poly drug abuse. It also does not mean that the person has two psychiatric disorders. Dual diagnosis means that there are two co-existing disorders. One is psychiatric and the other is addiction related.

Both the psychiatric and addiction components not only mask each other but also compound the degree of pathology.

The synergy created quadruples the degree of pathology. In the case of dual diagnosis, one plus one equals ten thousand. The interaction with the psychiatric disorder blows everything out of proportion. The interaction effects worsen each disorder. Alcoholism can cause the development of psychiatric and spiritual disorders as well as worsen existing disorders. Alcohol may cause psychiatric disorders that do not clear up when sober. If a person is vulnerable to psychiatric disorders, a few beers could cause severe depression.

It is difficult for trained clinicians to differentiate between the symptoms of each disorder. Imagine the difficulty for untrained, emotionally involved family members to clearly see what is going on. What an impossible task for the alcoholic with psychiatric disorders.

To the Christian, dual disorders include man's spiritual disorders. In the spiritual realm there are legitimate dual diagnosis cases. Sometimes severe chronic alcoholism is supported by a demonic infrastructure. An alcoholic who is demonically possessed has a dual diagnosis. The alcoholic may need deliverance to treat the possession and antabuse to treat the drunkenness. The maxim is that treatment must always be applied to the spiritual illness before the medical or psychological intervention.

## The Church's Complicity in Progression

The church has a responsibility to the alcoholic and drunk, which is often abdicated. The church is often guilty of the sin of omission concerning the alcoholic and drunk. There are things each denomination does to help but they all fall short of their mandate.

Years ago a good intentioned intercessor responded to an unsaved woman's request for prayer to heal her headache. Virtually everything he did was wrong because he did not have discernment. There were questions that needed to be asked. He did not ask what her reasons were for asking for prayer, especially since she was not a Christian. It seemed appropriate to question her about the cause of her headache. Was it because she read without her glasses? Was it a hangover? In fact she was very hung over. While laying hands on her head, this intercessor began to pray out loud. The intercessor was not praying in the Holy Spirit, but spoke a "word salad monologue." Just as it says in Corinthians, she left thinking the whole place was weird because the person spoke gibberish. The headache did not go away. Prescribing aspirin would have been more effective. This type of intercessor often enjoys the pride associated with being an intercessor, but wears that title loosely. Instead, he should have provided Christian counsel. At least good advice would not have scared her away from visiting at a later time.

There was a young Christian girl who lived in a small country town. The very first time she got drunk she overdosed and was rushed to the local emergency room. This happened on Friday night. When she woke up Saturday, she cried out to God in repentance and resolved never to drink again. On Sunday, as usual, she went to her church. Unfortunately, the church did not minister God's mercy and forgiveness. They did much more than rebuke her; they ostracized her and told her not to ever come back. She was shattered and missed church for over a decade. This congregation hurt her instead of helped her. Their sin caused this girl much psychological illness. She became a drug addict, overdosed, and died.

Alcoholics can prevent demons from having the advantage over them if they understand the methods used to damn them. The demon's success depends on secrecy. The church has authority and power over demons. It can set captive alcoholics free by making the demon's plans known. Unfortunately, there is a lack of knowledge in the church regarding demonic power and Christian authority. When pastoral guidance is absent, demons prosper.

# RELAPSE PREVENTION

The old maxim, "An ounce of prevention is worth a pound of cure," is the Wonderful Counselor's prescription of choice. Preventing drunkenness is a wonderful method of dealing with the ravages of Satan. Anyone burning in hell for drunkenness will testify to the importance of preventing sin.

Relapse prevention is different from treatment. Whereas treatment initiates change, relapse prevention maintains the change. Relapse prevention's goal is to increase the probability that drunkenness does not return once recovery has been initiated. Therefore, treatment interventions may not be very effective in preventing relapse. Completely new strategies are often needed to prevent relapse. Christian counsel may provide the impetus for an addict to repent but what will prevent the person from relapsing when under stress? This is the business of relapse prevention and aftercare.

Since sin is a part of life, aftercare is focused on resisting temptation. After the alcoholic repents of a sin, often the desire to recommit the sin is to some degree present. After the alcoholic repents of drunkenness, urges and craving to re-establish the sin are natural and can be triggered by many situations. Alcoholics must be taught the skills to avoid those triggers, or occasions of sin, and to quickly repent if the sin re-occurs, so as not to allow it to become a re-established behavior pattern. Relapse does not always happen because the sober alcoholic plans to drink, but rather, they make the error of not planning to avoid temptation. If the Christian alcoholic relapses he should immediately repent. If he relapses again and again he must immediately repent again and again. The conditioned response from trigger to behavior needs to be broken. The person contemplating a relapse into a previously repented sin may not even be consciously aware that they are contemplating it. The alcoholic must guard their sobriety by either avoiding triggers or by having a plan on how to deal with triggers when they spontaneously arise. Fortunately, to the skilled counselor the alcoholic manifests many warning signs. The relapse syndrome follows a degenerative process, which the counselor can perceive. For example, the alcoholic may begin to get unusually angry or argumentative or appear depressed.

## The Spiritual Steps to Relapse

The demons are annoyed that they have lost the soul of the newly sober alcoholic. They understand alcohol's value for destroying and damning souls. They know no better way to accomplish their diabolical agenda than by reactivating the alcoholic's drinking. It is much easier for them to tempt an alcoholic to drink than it is for them to tempt an alcoholic to commit murder or adultery. They know it is second nature for the alcoholic to drink and they know that one moment of drunkenness will cause separation from God.

The same conditions that cause drunkenness also cause the alcoholic in recovery to relapse. These conditions are the spiritual, physical, and psychological diseases of alcoholism. Coincidentally, since drunkenness is a sin, these same conditions are also the steps that result in the commission of a sin. The alcoholic can learn to recognize when they are subconsciously considering a relapse. Then they can implement an intervention before their first drink. There are four steps that result in the sin of drunkenness. They are: 1) the temptation; 2) meditation on the temptation; 3) sinning in the heart; and finally 4) the sinful behavior.

*Real Insight*

STEVEN KOPOR

**The First Step: The Temptation.**

The sober alcoholic is involved in constant spiritual warfare. Alcoholics do not necessarily need demonic temptation to motivate them to get drunk. Sometimes their own flesh or the spirit of the world in them causes them to get drunk. Relapse is not necessarily related to withdrawal symptoms. The temptation can arise even when the alcoholic feels great.

An increase in "stinking thinking" always precedes a lapse or relapse. The following are examples of the "stinking thinking" that run through the minds of all alcoholics during the early stages of sobriety. The alcoholic does not think that he will become a drunk again. He is like the drug addict who, as a teenager, dabbled with drugs, never thinking he would become a junkie. He believes he can drink in moderation. He plans to prove his resolve or test his control. Some think they can go to a bar, drink only soda, and socialize with their old drinking buddies. Others think relapse begins with the first drink. They assume that their relationship with God and family are wonderful. They make major life decisions with the false certainty that God directed them. During this time, delusion through euphoric recall sets in and they forget the reasons they stopped drinking. In fact, they really do not believe those reasons exist anymore. The devil tries to trick the sober alcoholic into believing that on rare occasions a lapse or relapse is exactly what the they need before they decide to completely abstain forever. The demonic argument is that a relapse would cause the alcoholic to learn about the emptiness of drinking. It would teach humility and dependence on God. It would make them more understanding and forgiving of others who relapse. The seeds of discontent begin to take root and grow as the dry drunk resents his decision to become sober. This type of thinking is fertile ground for demons to plant seeds of relapse.

This "stinking thinking" is a lie from hell. When alcoholics are being tempted and are seriously considering a relapse they should ask themselves, "What is the strongest indicator of having a full blown relapse?" It should be obvious that a lapse gives the strongest indication of a relapse. Therefore, lapses should be avoided like the plague.

The sober alcoholic is not usually aware that he is going to either lapse or relapse. He does not know why he drank. It was not premeditated, it was impulsive behavior. Consciously the drunk is innocent, but <u>there was a lot of subconscious scheming before the relapse</u>. <u>All sin, including drunkenness, begins long before the observable behavior</u>.

Relapse may also occur because the sober alcoholic cannot handle the reality of never drinking again. This is why it is important that recovery is done one day at a time.

**The Second Step: Meditation on the Temptation.**

When an alcoholic is unable to get the temptation to drink out of his mind he has not yet committed a sin, but the probability of relapse greatly increases. It is only a human weakness to dwell on temptation, not a sin. A temptation may enter the mind but stay only briefly because it finds no affection on which to bond. On the other hand, if upon entering the mind it finds affection, it stays and unites to the affection causing spiritual motion toward sin. Once temptation and affection unite, the gulf between temptation and sin is greatly decreased. The person who meditates on temptation conjures up mental images and dwells on the unholy. He begins to crave alcohol if drunkenness is the temptation. He dredges up sugar coated memories of prior drinking experiences. The temptation is reinforced by the positive emotions of euphoric recall. The pleasure further tempts the alcoholic to drink. Eventually, even the memory of drunkenness can cause craving, temptation, and relapse. As the alcoholic dwells on a temptation to drink he weakens his resolve for sobriety because he is conforming to the way of the world. Satan's degenerating process occurs to the degree that the person considers temptation. Hence, they build the scaffolding to support the temptation, making relapse very probable.

The proper Christian response to temptation is to immediately rebuke the thought and change the attention to another thought. The temptation should not be dwelled upon, so as to activate the emotions and somatic responses, but immediately be dismissed. In order to increase the probability of preventing relapse, there is great value in changing the "stinking thinking" to what is good and virtuous. The easiest way is to develop the habit of instantly replacing it with a planned prayer. The prayer, "Lord have mercy on me a sinner," is very helpful. Express to God your sorrow for offending Him. When Jesus was tempted He did not dwell on the thought. Jesus did more than merely renounce the thought. Using scripture He renounced Satan, the source of the thought.

**The Third Step: Deciding in the Heart.**

The alcoholic becomes guilty of sin when he allows the temptation to enter into his mind, meditates on it, and decides in his heart to commit the sin. Sin occurs because the alcoholic responds to temptation by condoning the demonic urge rather than resisting it.

The best illustration to demonstrate this can be found in Matthew 5:28 when Jesus said, "But I tell you that anyone who looks at a woman lustfully has already committed adultery with her in his heart." Even though the physical act of adultery was not committed, a sin took place. This illustrates that the alcoholic can commit drunkenness in his heart without drinking. The sin is committed when the alcoholic's mind, will, and emotions are in communion. There is no conflict; only the desire, commitment, drive, and plan to get drunk. The alcoholic demonstrates motive and intent to God. The person who spends all night trying to buy drugs but cannot find a place to purchase them is as guilty of sin as the person trying to commit adultery but cannot because of lack of opportunity. To God, sin is obviously a matter of heart, not only behavior. Most dry drunks are drunks at heart. They commit the sin of drunkenness without drinking.

### The Fourth Step: The Lapse or Relapse.

Acting out the heart's desire in thought is virtually as evil as acting it out in behavior, but the biological consequences of drunkenness do not occur because no psychoactive substance was ingested.

The alcoholic who relapses has placed himself under the dominion of the demons. He has sold his soul, at least temporarily, to the demons. He rejected the cross of sobriety and returned to slavery. The demons try to lessen the perception of wrongdoing and increase the perception of pleasure so that the alcoholic will continue to get drunk.

## Changing the Natural Progression of Alcoholism

As there are different fruits of the Holy Spirit, there are also different fruits of sin. That is the reason all sinners do not suffer the same diseases. A disease's chronicity, its progression, and the ill person's response are factors that control its course. Once a disease is established, feedback mechanisms contribute to its variations and longevity. Reinforcing causes prolong the duration of illness longer than its natural course.

When a person contracts a disease there are many possible illness patterns and outcomes. One outcome is the natural course of the disease without treatment. A different outcome could occur by rearranging variables so that the alternative future best suits the sick person and least suits the demons. For example, when a person breaks his leg, it is set and then it heals correctly. The natural course, without intervention, would be lameness. When a drunk offends someone, reconciliation can restore the relationship. The natural course without intervention would be a damaged relationship. The effects of an intervention often improve the alcoholic. Depending on the type of intervention, any number of different outcomes could occur.

When a child is brought up by Christian parents in a Christian home, and sent to a good Christian school, only God knows all the maladies in spirit, soul, and body that this upbringing prevented. Conversely, what about the child brought up in a non-Christian home? As the child grows he does not understand forgiveness or prayer. His capacity to resist temptation is greatly diminished. Only God knows all the maladies in spirit, body, and soul this child will experience throughout his life.

In God's mercy, there are interventions that can change the course of the worst drunk's life. Through prayer even an evil wicked drunk could be converted at age 70, baptized, filled with the Holy Spirit, and live a good Christian life. The intervention of becoming a Christian changed the course of his life. His final destination after physical death becomes heaven instead of hell. Any drunk who begins recovery can experience this type of drastic change.

## Prevention of the Sin of Drunkenness

When most people think of prevention they are thinking of intervention before the onset of an illness to ensure that the illness never occurs. Divine health is better than divine healing. It aims to establish the necessary conditions, which reduce the incidence of illness occurring. It focuses on eliminating the cause (demonic aggression, sin, lack of exercise, poor diet), strengthening the host (prayer, exercise, fasting, vaccinations, baptism) and eradicating the negative environmental factors (cursed objects, toxic environment). At the spiritual level, praying for a child while the mother is pregnant, Christian education, and avoiding occasions of sin are examples of this level of prevention. At the psychological level, teaching decision-making and coping skills are examples of primary prevention. At the biological level, vaccinations, early screening of children, and neonatal medicine are examples. Unfortunately, most interventionists, whether the minister, counselor, or physician, view their task as combating illness.

Until the return of Christ, sickness will be part of the nature of man. The best that man can hope for is to prevent sickness or to quickly cure it when it occurs. The second level of prevention calls for early detection of disorders before any permanent damage occurs. It is prevention in that it prevents an existing illness from becoming chronic, through prompt treatment. Thus it shortens the duration of illnesses. For example, unrepented sin tends to motivate the soul to commit more sin. Repentance prevents the recurrence of sin.

As can be seen, the prevention/treatment dichotomy breaks down. Prevention and treatment are not separate things but parts of a whole, with intervention being the whole. The behaviors prescribed by Jesus, which prevent illness often serve as treatment. Prayer, fasting, Bible study, and meditation are equally powerful in the prevention and treatment of alcoholism.

The third level of prevention is synonymous with relapse prevention and aftercare. It helps the alcoholic adjust to the permanent effects of the disease. It is a noble work to pray for these cases, but there comes a time when hope shatters and the alcoholic is confronted with a permanent disability. At this point it is appropriate to teach them to pray for the strength and courage to live with an illness instead of praying for healing. Relapse prevention aims to teach the alcoholic that despite chronic impairment, he can have a peaceful recovery.

## Restrictions on Demons

The demons' ability to wield their power is limited by the parameters established by God. If God did not limit Satan and his demons, the human condition would be much worse than it is. They would instantly kill all those who fall into deadly sin, and send them to hell. Demons could wipe mankind off the face of the earth but God prevents this. God established laws, which limit how and under which conditions demons can attack man. Satan could not torment Job until God gave him permission. God limited Satan's attacks to those outside of Job's body. Satan could only do to Job what God allowed, nothing more. Job was protected because God restricted Satan. In Job 2:3-7, God allowed Satan to escalate his fury and he attacked Job in the form of illness. Not only are limits imposed, but within the cap of attack the intensity of demonic aggression is under God's control.

The prayer Jesus prayed on the eve of His death has provided man with much protection against demons and sin (John 17:11, 17:15). Jesus prayed that God would deliver mankind from temptation. His prayer for our protection is very powerful and binds demons.

In 1 Corinthians 10:13, Peter declares that Christians can never be tempted beyond their limit. God will not allow the alcoholic's temptation to be greater than they can bear, but He will allow it to get right at the line. The alcoholic must be vigilant because the devil roams the Earth like a lion looking to devour. Alcoholics in recovery are a particularly tasty delight in addition to being an easy mark. Satan does not want the drunk to know that when he is resisted he must leave. All recovering alcoholics are tempted to drink and must choose to take God's escape route.

When temptation is resisted and prompts prayer to God, the demons eventually learn that temptation is counter-productive to their goals and they will retreat. Resisted temptation always builds character, brings the soul into closer union with God, and gives added strength to resist future temptation. It does not weaken a soul. It purifies the soul like fire purifies gold. The alcoholic has proven himself in battle. The Christian who prays and asks God to deliver them from temptation puts works behind their faith.

**Unregenerated Human Character**

Through man's God-given human nature, all mankind possesses a natural resistance to demonic aggression. God imprints His character into mankind's soul at conception. Mankind's free will provides much protection. Unfortunately, since the fall of man this power is greatly reduced. Even the drunk possesses this natural resistance, but to a lesser degree than even the alcoholic. Without the imprint of God's image and likeness, the demons would be more victorious.

Since the reason the Son of God became manifest was to destroy demonic works, man is inherently defended in spirit, soul, and body. If man applies the resources available to his soul, the devil's aggression can be deflected.

When compared to the spiritual defenses the psychological are like a hill compared to a mountain. The psychological defense mechanisms are a reflection of the spiritual defense mechanisms that energize them. Spiritual defenses establish the infrastructure for particular psychological defenses. There are natural healthy defense mechanisms, which God has established in man. Defense mechanisms generally serve a healthy purpose, but not when they are used by the disease of alcoholism. This spiritual defense structure is man's first line of defense against demonic attacks. The spiritual defense mechanisms give man the capacity to resist demonic aggression. Spiritual defense mechanisms are to psychological defense mechanisms as ears that hear and eyes that see are to natural perception. They establish the infrastructure for particular psychological defenses as opposed to others.

## Christian Character

Once a person becomes a genuine Christian they receive an infused new character, which automatically prevents much sin, but this is only the beginning. God's grace further adds to man's natural resistance by giving him grace, spiritual gifts, and virtues that prevent relapse. Each piece of the armor of Christ is a spiritual defense (Ephesians 6:12-18). The Christian's weapons are not worldly and they have divine power to destroy strongholds of Satan (2 Corinthians 10:3-4). The alcoholic begins to think of spiritual things, not carnal (Colossians 3:2). They think about truth, whatever is noble, right, pure, lovely, admirable, excellent, and praiseworthy (Philippians 4:8). They put off their old nature and are renewed in the Spirit (Ephesians 4:22-24). They do not conform to the world but are transformed by the renewal of their minds by presenting their bodies as a living sacrifice (Romans 12:2). This means that the alcoholic stops dwelling on getting drunk.

## Evangelism to the Drunken Alcoholic

Spreading the Gospel to the world is the best method to promote spiritual, psychological, and physiological health. Evangelism is more than preaching the Good News to people who have not heard it. In the spiritual realm it is the geographic displacement of demons.

On a global scale, evangelism is an instrument of healing for demonically possessed land. In non-Christian lands where idolatry reigns, and where man's old nature is not replaced, demonic aggression, demonic possession, as well as physical and mental illness are rampant. As a country becomes Christianized the leagues of unclean and unseen spirits who were moving about freely become bound. Demonic success is impeded by the higher number of Christians per capita. Being bound in a land causes the demons to migrate to a land where they can more freely move about. Demons have been severely limited by evangelism. Their control in Christian lands usually occurs at the perimeter of the geographical boundaries between Christendom and heathen lands. Within Christian lands there is limited demonic activity with an unusually high percentage of demonic activity concentrated in the psychiatric hospitals.

## Training Children to be Sober Adults

The timing of an intervention is as important as the type of intervention. The earlier the better. Therefore the best timing for intervention is prenatal, through prayer. Training involves teaching children not to sin, how to avoid occasions of sin, and how to avoid impulse motivated sin. These skills are very helpful in resisting the temptation to get drunk. Through training, parents take offensive action. Children need to learn how to live (Proverbs 22:6). If they are taught well, they will remember it all of their life. As the child grows into an adult, he must put away childish things. Children have to be taught how to think for themselves. An adult who, as a child was not taught to think for himself, is a slave and in bondage.

Parents need to teach by example and practice what they preach. Godly role modeling is important. Children do not need to grow up observing an inconsistency between what they see and what they are told to do. In the "good old days" a child grew up observing a consistent message from parents, school, and church. Today the child raised in a good home often experiences conflicting observations between home, school, and church, if he goes to church at all. This is another reason parents should not forsake the assembling of themselves together at church, for the children who go with them. If a child is raised devoutly in the church, he is less likely to become a drunk. The child should grow up evaluating life's circumstances according to Godly standards. If the disease of alcoholism is present it will most likely remain dormant.

It is the parent's responsibility to protect their children from the wiles of demons, the perversity of man, and accidents. Ultimately it is the parent's responsibility to protect their children, even from themselves. The sins inflicted on children by their drunken parents are often debilitating.

### Preventing Occasions of Sin

There are biblical precedents, which indicate that the avoidance of sin can lead to health. In Exodus 15:26, 23:25 and Deuteronomy 7:12-16, God declared to His people that He would not put the diseases He gave to the Egyptians on them if they would truly obey Him. Proverbs 3:7-8 states that those who obey God would be healthy. Conversely, there will be tribulation and distress for those who do evil, if not in this world then in the next.

Some alcoholics naively enter dangerous situations. If they knew the deadly implications of their behavior they would not get involved. Therefore, a sound Christian education can prevent relapse.

Drunkenness itself is an occasion of sin because it intrinsically has the power to cause sin. When a person, place, or thing has the power to allure and entice to sin, voluntary exposure to them is an occasion of sin. Working in a bar, brewery, or liquor store are occasions of sin. Socializing in a bar is a very dangerous occasion of sin. These occasions of sin are called "triggers" in the addiction literature. They activate the addiction.

All alcoholics should learn how to avoid the places and situations that could lead to relapse. When alcoholics deliberately put themselves into a position that could trigger temptation they are playing into the hands of the demons. The repentant alcoholic should not immediately try to convert his former drinking buddies. The Christian alcoholic who goes to a bar, even if he plans not to drink, is responsible for any temptation he gets. This type of temptation is never a sign of spiritual progress but is rather a sign of spiritual error. The conversion process is spiritual warfare and a new Christian can mistake temptation for inspiration. God provides a way to escape temptation, but they compulsively seek it out. No wonder they are experiencing the desire for alcohol.

**Protection From the Sins of Others**

Anybody can be the victim of the sins of another person. The child molester's sin hurts its young victim. The rapist's sin often leaves emotional scars throughout the victim's life. The thief's sin deprives the victim of property. Generational curses are passed down to children. The effects of sin inflicted onto another may cause permanent damage.

Even when the victim can manage to forgive the perpetrator, the stain in their soul may remain for life. The Christian alcoholic must learn strategies to protect himself from the temptations of man and demons.

**Sins of the Scientific Health Professionals**

There are secular healing techniques that cause spiritual, psychological, and/or physical damage to the alcoholic. Medical research, especially experimental drugs or procedures, often damages the subject. These are generally benevolent attempts to update medical technology but demons also inspire diabolical medical and psychological research done in the name of science. Demons also inspire perverted health professionals to commit acts that are not condoned by other professionals. This is the physical, sexual, and/or emotional abuse which some secretly inflict on helpless patients.

Inside treatment facilities there are sinful activities which worsen the alcoholic's illness. These are the sins that the patients inflict upon each other. Often an alcoholic goes into a treatment facility with their own problems, but through their association with the other alcoholics they come out with more problems than when they went in. The Bible teaches that evil companions corrupt good character (1 Corinthians 15:33).

**Alcoholics Must Avoid All Forms of Hypnotism**

It is wrong to use hypnotism for treatment because it is an occult technique used to develop occult powers. Hypnotism has been used by occultists for millenniums. Those who practice fortune telling or divination have practiced some form of hypnotism. Many of the professionals who use hypnotism believe it is a useful treatment method. They disclaim or minimize its occult connection. Therefore, they have no reservation about using this satanic treatment method. Secular therapies, which use hypnosis, are occult sciences. An occult technique has spread from the obviously occult to the sublimely occult. An alcoholic who has been hypnotized will probably need deliverance from the demons that entered during hypnosis before Christian counseling can proceed.

Alcohol deludes the drunk by creating pseudo spirituality. The drunk progresses through several stages before he becomes a falling down, slobbering, babbling idiot. The first drink primes the demonic pump. It explodes like a gusher and quickly spirals the drunk's life downward to create a weapon for evil. They feel so much stress until they gulp that first, second, and third drink. By the fourth drink they are feeling normal. It is while drinking the fifth, sixth, seventh, and eighth drink that many drunks begin to experience a hypnotic pseudo spirituality. This experience is drug induced and very pagan. They enter that altered state of consciousness in which demons love to dwell. The drunk experiences feelings of closeness with God when in actuality the sin of drunkenness has separated him from God. Now he has great resolve to recommit his life to God. He plans to pray more, read the Bible more, and generally dedicate himself to God. He makes plans to attend church. Soon though, he has had his tenth, fifteenth, etc., drink; all his resolve is washed away and a type of demonic possession overtakes him. His resolve dissolves. The next day he often does not even remember what he did. He goes to bed drunk and wakes up repentant, only to repeat the process every day.

When drunk, alcoholics are in a hypnotic state which makes them much more open to suggestion than when sober. It is bad enough that they listen to their drunken friends, but worse, they become more open to demonic suggestion. As the disease progresses they become more open to demonic suggestion even when sobor.

One of the chronic consequences of drunkenness is that it damages the sober alcoholic's ability to meditate. Alcohol creates a semi-hypnotic state, not a meditative state. For some alcoholics, the altered consciousness of meditation can open the alcoholic to demonic influences. It can lead to relapse and eternal damnation.

# THE DRY DRUNK SYNDROME

## The Development of the Dry Drunk

Immediately after hitting bottom, most alcoholics are happy to be sober. This is because the problems associated with sobriety have not yet begun. At this point all sober alcoholics share a common experience in their physical healing. They all begin to detox. This is the end of any similarities in recovery. Sober alcoholics develop into one of two distinct groups about their potential for successful recovery and spiritual progress. After the honeymoon of sobriety wears off, the state of being which will accompany the alcoholic through the rest of his sober life begins to develop. At this point, there begins a differentiation in the psychological and spiritual processes, which cause the sober alcoholic to either become a dry drunk or begin Christian recovery. Their decision to become sober is based on different motivations, reasons, and emotions. They also react differently to the stresses of sobriety. Most importantly, the spiritual differentiation takes the Christian alcoholic along one path and the dry drunk along another.

The first group is the recovering Christian alcoholics who will achieve sobriety and serenity. To ensure a successful recovery the Christian alcoholic must implement a spiritual treatment component. The Christian method is the easiest, quickest, and surest way to prevent relapse or the dry drunk syndrome. How to begin Christian recovery and make spiritual progress is fully discussed later.

The second group is the dry drunks. Dry drunks merely transform from being wet drunks to dry drunks. It is second nature for the dry drunk to become a wet drunk again. Their addicted thinking remains intact. Those who begin sobriety, minus recovery, live as dry drunks until they relapse. Dry drunks never begin recovery, but only sobriety. Those who enter recovery may lapse but they never relapse. Only dry drunks relapse. Although some dry drunks relapse after twenty years of sobriety, the majority relapse within the first few months. Sobriety should get easier as time increases, but this is not true for the dry drunk.

Unfortunately, the dry drunk either neglects or refuses to practice the Christian method. This is an especially vulnerable time and the demons understand this weak link in the recovery process. The demons try to turn all sober alcoholics into dry drunks while the Holy Spirit hopes all sober alcoholics begin Christian recovery. Is it any wonder demons deceive the reformed drunk at this important fork on the road? After sobriety, this is the first serious battle in the spiritual war. The Christian alcoholic begins recovery while the dry drunk stays sober but otherwise makes very little progress.

Living as a dry drunk is not as bad as being a drunken alcoholic, but when compared to the many devout and holy Christian alcoholics who are making spiritual progress, the dry drunk's sobriety is inferior. Some dry drunks think they are practicing the Christian faith in their recovery, but they are fooling themselves. They are certainly good intentioned, but the road to hell is paved with good intentions. What they practice is superficial or hypocritical.

There are many problems related to drunkenness, which continue well into sobriety. The joy of sobriety quickly fades as the dry drunk realizes that his life is still very difficult. Even during the brief moments of passing joy they are consciously aware of their discomfort without alcohol. They assumed that when they stopped drinking things would quickly get better. They are surprised by the effort involved in remaining sober. The misery of the dry drunk is one of the triggers for relapse. At this point in sobriety they are still reaping the consequences of their drunken lifestyle. The principle of seed time and harvest time is in operation even though they may have repented and been forgiven. The consequences of their drunken behavior need time to work themselves out. People may still be angry with them, they may have employment problems, or they may be in litigation over some alcohol-related crime. If the sober alcoholic is still experiencing psychological problems after one year of sobriety he is well established on the road to becoming a dry drunk. Psychological disorders also increase the probability of relapse.

The quick fix of alcohol is especially appealing to the dry drunk whose life is a perpetual hell. It appears that all the fury of hell is released and focused on them. They have to deal with the painful psychological problems of their alcoholism without its sedative effects. A torrent of repressed and suppressed emotions enters consciousness like a raging volcano. The dry drunk's desire for alcohol exponentially increases, while the Christian alcoholic in recovery experiences a lessening of the desire to drink. If the dry drunk manages to remain sober, he will constantly fight the desire to drink.

The dry drunk has an unconscious desire to be drunk despite an incongruent conscious belief that he wants to abstain. The conscious part of his dilemma is that he is sober and he knows he hates it. He also unconsciously opposes any prudent behavior that would promote sobriety. The dry drunk deliberately seeks out those activities that tend to make sobriety more difficult to maintain. This unconscious bondage makes the sober alcoholic a genuine dry drunk. Dry drunks never let go of the addictive alcoholic personality even through they stopped drinking.

The dry drunk's long term sobriety is not much different than the short term sobriety he experienced in between waking up after a heavy night of drinking and his next day's first drink. To them, the tenth year of sobriety is as difficult as the first few days. The dysfunctional behaviors exhibited by the dry drunk are a moderate form of his drunken behavior; therefore the similarities trigger identical emotional conditioned responses. The dysfunctional behavior of the dry drunk is an indicator of the ever-present disease of alcoholism. When a sober alcoholic acts and feels the same as he did during his drinking days, he will soon relapse.

## A Dry Drunk Parable

The dry drunk is like a person beginning a race with a long bungee cord tied to him and the other end tied to the starting pole. As the race begins, the cord is not a hindrance since it has slack. Soon, the cord is stretching and actually slowing the runner's progress because of the extra effort needed to offset the resistance caused by the stretched cord. The further the runner gets from the start pole, the more the cord stretches and causes greater resistance. Eventually, the cord reaches its maximum stretched length. The runner will be hindered from going any further, no matter how much effort is exerted. For a while the runner will exert maximum effort but only be running in place. As the runner weakens, the pull from the cord will begin to draw him back to the starting pole.

When the drunk actually becomes sober, he is like the person tied to the start pole with a bungee cord. The bungee cord represents the psychological, physical and spiritual baggage he takes with him on the journey of sobriety. The stretched cord pulling the runner backwards represents the diseased "stinking thinking." The stretching cord also represents the stress they experience. As the dry drunk's days of sobriety increase, so does his pathological desire to drink. With great speed the alcoholic relapses. If he actually continues to refrain, he is miserable and a bad example to other drunks who wish to begin recovery.

## The Dry Drunk's Spiritual Attachment to Alcohol

Once the alcoholic becomes sober he has taken the first step on the road of spiritual progress and recovery. The second step in the process is to lose or diminish the attachment to drunkenness. Unless this is accomplished the sober alcoholic will be a dry drunk. The dry drunk must lose his spiritual attachment to drunkenness otherwise the temptation to drink will obsess his thoughts until he relapses.

Dry drunks may have stopped drinking, but they still love to get drunk. Dry drunks could be sober for 20 years and be in constant spiritual warfare over whether or not to have a drink. Although they have stopped drinking, they have not lost the attachment to that sin within their hearts. They are still slaves to alcohol. When the dry drunk expresses the desire to be a social drinker, this is evidence he has not lost his attachment to the sin of drunkenness.

When a drunk gives up alcohol, he is giving up more than drinking. Most of his life revolved around alcohol while he was a drunk. It's no wonder he does not want to completely sever his relationship with alcohol. To the drunk, alcohol is one of his most intimate friends. Alcohol has seen him through many of his life's problems. Alcohol was there during much of his development. He has run to alcohol for help in coping with life's stresses. If he were not drunk or getting drunk, he was either working to draw a salary to purchase alcohol, or being hung over, or worrying about some drunken behavior, or experiencing a consequence of drunkenness. The anxiety of separation causes grief just as it would if a friend died or moved away.

Attachment in the soul toward anything but God can be an obstacle to spiritual progress. Even when the object of attachment is morally neutral or otherwise good, excessive attachment is dangerous. If attachment toward morally good things can be a source of danger, what about attachment to the mortal sin of drunkenness? Attachment to the mortal sin of drunkenness is the primary cause of relapse.

## Dry Drunks Are Sober for Worldly, Not Spiritual Reasons

There are many spiritual reasons alcoholics choose to completely abstain from alcohol. The highest, most perfect reason is simply love of God. The second best reason is obedience to God's will. It is also good to stop because drunken behavior hurts those closest to them. It is also valuable to abstain because of the confusion it can cause in weaker Christians or because of the wrong idea it can give to the world.

Dry drunks have not stopped because of love of God or any other spiritual motivation. They practice sobriety for worldly reasons. The dry drunk's sobriety is only to escape dire consequences, fear of cirrhosis, divorce, or jail, etc. Simply, the dry drunk wants to be drunk, but the fear of the consequences outweighs the desire to drink. When the reason for sobriety is externally imposed, the alcoholic will be miserable and prone to relapse. They are being compelled to stop against their will. They hate it and resent being forced.

Some practice sobriety to manipulate God, as if this were possible. They believe God's blessings are contingent on how they act. This is why it is hard for the drunk, even when sober, to develop a healthy relationship with God. Their relationship with God is to further their own selfish ends. When sobriety is motivated by the wrong reasons, the person is a dry drunk.

Unfortunately, many alcoholics do the right thing for the wrong reason. To get the most grace, the alcoholic needs to do the right thing for the right reason. Without the right motivation all outward deeds, even noble and virtuous, are less meritorious. Therefore, sobriety for the wrong reason is spiritually of less value.

Very few drunken alcoholics want to stop drinking for noble, spiritual reasons. Whatever the drunken alcoholic's motive to abstain, praise God! Whatever the drunk's motives are, it is better to abstain than to be a drunken alcoholic. If they would only decide to stop drinking for love of God, then His abundant grace would fill their spirit and spill over into their body and mind. Recovery and spiritual progress would be swift.

## Dry Drunks Practice Idolatry

Drunks practice idolatry. Since dry drunks are drunks at heart, they also commit idolatry. Their idolatry does not manifest in the worship of a statue or participation in a pagan temple. Yet, the same mental state that operates in the pagan worship of statues operates in them. The only difference is the object of their idolatry. They substitute alcohol and drunkenness for statues. They do not realize alcohol is their deity. They may believe Jesus is God but even the demons believe Jesus is God. Jesus is not the Lord of their life; alcohol is the lord of their life. It's idolatry because dry drunks worship and serve alcohol instead of God. They would sell their soul to get drunk.

Their idolatry takes form in the love of drunkenness and the reverence they bestow on it. They offer worship to their idol by offering sacrifices to it. They willingly place their family, career, and worse, their relationship with the true God on the altar of sacrifice. They give up all, including eternal life, for their god.

Alcoholics replace God with alcohol whether they consciously realize it or not. It is idolatry because they truly believe that alcohol is a better wellspring of life than God. Alcohol is raised to a place of esteem far above God. They use alcohol to meet the needs God should meet. God is reduced to being used when they want to be enabled. Otherwise, it is alcohol, not God, who they depend on and commune with.

Alcohol freely receives the surrender of self. The self should die in Christ, not be strangled to death by alcohol. In the case of the drunk and the dry drunk, the surrender of self is to the demonic. They give to alcohol that part of themselves which rightfully belongs to God. It is idolatry because they use alcohol to fill that exact same part of the soul that is God's domain. As it is true a person cannot love money and God, it is equally true that they cannot love alcohol and God.

When they repent and begin Christian recovery, Jesus happily unites with them and fills the void caused by the exorcism of the false god of alcohol. The dry drunk does not exorcise their false God of drunkenness.

## Dry Drunks Have a Psychological Awakening, Not a Spiritual Awakening

Dry drunks experience a psychological awakening, not a spiritual one. Since the dry drunk does not experience a spiritual awakening, they are not in recovery. The spiritual awakening is itself a necessary milestone to initiate recovery. Sobriety without a spiritual awakening is also insufficient to guarantee continued sobriety.

The drunk who sobers up through only a psychological awakening is doomed to be a dry drunk. As a general rule, dry drunks do not place much emphasis on the spiritual aspects of their sobriety. They do not practice the spiritual disciplines that contribute to a peaceful recovery. Dry drunks never experience true peace and serenity because these come as a result of a deep spiritual life. The psychologically awakened alcoholic only practices futility because the driving force behind their drunkenness, the disease of alcoholism, is fully active. Psychologically awakened alcoholics progress slowly and awkwardly in their sobriety. Therefore, they have a higher chance to relapse. They are in the precarious situation of shortly becoming slaves of the devil through drunkenness or through the living hell of being a dry drunk.

On the other hand, the spiritually awakened alcoholic is fully aware of God's grace working in their recovery. When recovery begins with a spiritual awakening, the alcoholic has the greatest chance of genuinely being healed. It is this spiritual awakening which opens the door for the Christian alcoholic to receive abundant healing grace into his heart. The recovering Christian alcoholic gets spiritual power, which comes through a spiritual awakening. Devout activities are very important, but the difference between a dry drunk and a happy recovering alcoholic is determined by whether or not he has had a spiritual awakening.

It is the rare psychologically-awakened sober alcoholic who loses his attachment to drunkenness and avoids becoming a dry drunk. The psychologically- awakened dry drunk may attend church but he is spiritually disabled. It is grace from God that is the missing factor in the dry drunk's sobriety. Until he acquires this grace he will remain a dry drunk.

There are two types of spiritual awakenings. The best spiritual awakening for successful recovery takes place within a Christian context. The alcoholic's chances of recovery increase when he experiences a spiritual awakening, is born again, and experiences the inner transformation of becoming a new creature in Christ. It is the beginning of spiritual formation, which is blessed by God.

On the other hand, a spiritual awakening into an occult or new age spiritual system is itself a source of cursing. A non-Christian spiritual formation bestows much less or possibly no grace on the sober alcoholic. If a baptized Christian who, through drunkenness, fell away from God begins a non-Christian spiritual formation process, he is still in mortal sin.

## The Dry Drunk's Recovery is Based on Works, Not Faith

Faith is not just a confident belief in a body of knowledge. This type of faith justifies present beliefs by accepting the past. The alcoholic has to do something with the faith delivered to the saints, not merely recall it. The faith the alcoholic uses to become sober is a proactive faith. It transforms passive intentions into active willingness. It is a confident expectation of future recovery. Through faith the alcoholic crosses over into the supernatural realm, grabs hold of a healing, and pulls it back to this side of reality. Unfortunately, some alcoholics cannot reach across the veil and pull from the body of faith. When they attempt it, they reach a void where the content of their faith is useless as a wellspring to support recovery.

All alcoholics accomplish sobriety through a combination of faith and works, but the proportion of faith and works are different. When faith is the predominant factor the grace bestowed on the alcoholic promotes recovery. When works are the predominant factor the sober alcoholic is usually miserable and a dry drunk. Faith generates a perpetual supply of willpower, while the willpower generated from works quickly diminishes.

The alcoholic's faith must have Jesus as its source and content. The alcoholic in recovery has faith in Christ, but the dry drunk does not. What the alcoholic believes has a lot of control over his sobriety. The alcoholic's lack of faith in Jesus limits his chances of success. The dry drunk's abstinence is commendable but it is accomplished through his own nature, not God's grace; by works, not faith. They mistake their effort as being the sole source of their sobriety. The dry drunk does not think he owes his sobriety to God's mercy. When obstacles on the road to recovery are reached, the dry drunk believes it was his own internal resources that got him through the tough times. When the alcoholic attempts to stop drinking by his own willpower he is acting out a rebellious self sufficiency which offends God. The attitude of self sufficiency is always a precipitant to a relapse.

Sometimes the dry drunk relies on works, not faith, but truly believes that he is relying on God. He talks as if he trusts in God and His providence, but every step he takes proves otherwise. The alcoholic can ensure his acts of recovery are done in faith if he acts only under the prompting of the Holy Spirit. This motive rules out the motivation of self-reliance, which produces works-based sobriety. They have to learn to love, adore, and praise God because this type of thinking has the side effect of creating and empowering their faith. There is an awesome synergism generated by the combination of faith and works.

## Dry Drunks Experience Behavioral Not Spiritual Change

The dry drunk, like the hypocritical Pharisee, practices external behaviors without the corresponding internal spiritual dispositions. Although the Pharisees looked pious to the casual observer, they were full of evil. When external religious acts are committed which are not inspired by grace, there is little, if any, benefit. Indeed, Jesus criticized those who prayed or fasted for public glory. The dry drunk, although sober, is really full of the same internal drunkenness as when he was actually a drunk. The reason a dry drunk who abstained for decades begins to drink as if he never stopped is because he remained a drunk at heart, only his drinking behavior disappeared. While it is true that his drinking habits are different, it is untrue that there has been change in his spiritual or psychological makeup. Dry drunks do not possess that inner transformation into holiness but are merely focused on the superficial exterior act of abstinence. The external practice of abstinence merely gives the appearance of inward change. They love to get drunk and are barely refraining.

Dry drunks do not measure their progress by internal spiritual and psychological improvement. They focus on exterior practices like abstinence or attendance at Twelve Step meetings as indications of their progress. They can recite a few prayers and clichés but inwardly they are in need of healing. They confuse abstinence with progress toward holiness. In reality, abstinence is only the first milestone on a long road of healing. It is the least they could do. Practicing sobriety is practically worthless unless the person simultaneously carries his daily cross, reforms his life, and purifies his soul.

Sobriety is good, but when it consists exclusively of outward behaviors without any corresponding internal healing it becomes dangerous. It lulls the alcoholic to sleep with self satisfaction while it impairs the desire for genuine spiritual progress. They seem to be clothed in the virtue of temperance but inwardly they are mean, nasty, repressed drunks. The dry drunk may even appear to be making progress, but just below the surface there is an entirely different dysfunctional alcoholic personality. The dry drunk can actually go backwards in his spiritual development. The dry drunk could go to hell because he goes through the form of religion without a spiritual connection to God.

When alcoholics stop drinking they still have many disease processes in place which can cause a relapse. As soon as they relapse the disease causes their evil nature to quickly erupt and take control. They quickly transform into the beasts they were when a drunk. This happens because they never experienced a spiritual change.

## Dry Drunks Are Spiritual But Not Religious

Christians in recovery should realize that Jesus went to church. He knew the problems of the institutional church and testified to its faults, nevertheless, he attended church. He even preached in church. Jesus understood the need of the church in the world so he established the Christian church, which spiritualists reject. All recovering Christian alcoholics should imitate and follow Jesus. The spiritualist is theologically incorrect. If spiritualists were not against religion but merely against hypocritical practices, they would be in agreement with Jesus since he, too, rebuked the Pharisees. When alcoholics say that they are spiritual but not religious, most mean they do not want to go to church. When an alcoholic rejects religion, they reject God and His church. God established religion, but they say to hell with it. Alcoholics cannot be truly spiritual if they are prejudiced against religion because God put religion and spirituality inseparably together. They have disassociated themselves from God by denying the expression of their spiritually through His Majesty's church. They do not know true spirituality because this consists of knowing and doing the Father's will and they are not going to His church.

The spiritualists claim that recovery and spiritual progress are not dependent on organized religion. This is simply not true. The saints who practiced religion were not deceived. The saints practiced their religion devoutly and were more spiritual than most. They were certainly more spiritual than the dry drunks who are spiritual but not religious. Those who claim to be spiritual but not religious are really saying that they know better than the collective Christian church.

The spiritual but not religious belief is one of the most effective tools demons use to keep alcoholics miserable. It is God's church, spirituality and religion combined, that gives the recovering alcoholic the power to resist the devil's temptation of relapse. The alcoholic who is spiritual but not religious separates himself from a lot of grace at a critical period in his sobriety. It only serves the demons when a sober alcoholic does not belong to a church. Since drunkenness is a spiritual disease, those who reject religion are at a great disadvantage in their recovery from alcohol.

This is a very dangerous situation for the alcoholic since the demons can more easily pick off the isolated. Without religion, spiritual formation is easily manipulated by demons. Demons are less inclined to use their limited resources on the alcoholic who has a fully integrated spiritual/religious development, when they can attack someone weaker and unprotected. Since demons are economical in their diabolical efforts to destroy the alcoholic, the rejection of religion meets their needs. It only makes sense that the straight path of recovery is more easily trodden by the alcoholic who is in a good church.

If the alcoholic attended church before he became a drunk, his drunkenness distorted his understanding of religion. This is evident by his subsequent rejection of religion. His mind became clouded and his understanding of religion actually deteriorated. The alcoholic's view of religion becomes distorted because of progressive demonic shaping. Demons have wreaked such havoc in his mind that he does not know how to be religious. At first the drunk stops attending church because he is too hung over, wants to drink on Sunday morning or is simply too lazy to get up and go out in public. He makes excuses, for example, that the services are too long, it is boring, or the church is full of hypocrites. Often during the course of their active alcoholism they have been emotionally hurt by the people comprising the church. Maybe the pastor was not available when they needed help. Maybe the church ostracized them for always being drunk. Possibly someone sat in their favorite seat. The drunk will generalize their anger, which should be directed at an individual to the church and religion in general. Often alcoholics are so deeply hurt by such small things that they are unable to renew their relationship with the organized church. There are millions of possible scenarios that have been played out between the drunk and the church. The demons make alcoholics overreact in such ways that they voluntarily remove themselves from the source of grace most necessary for their personal recovery. Eventually, drunks rationalize their lack of church attendance. They think that they do not need to go to church to have a meaningful relationship with God. Without restoration to the organized church, most alcoholics will become dry drunks.

    The only reason alcoholics become spiritual and not religious is because it is much easier for demons to destroy their religion than their spirituality. It is the demonic goal to destroy spirituality as well as religion, but to destroy a soul's spirituality requires much more abuse. This is because spirituality is an infused instinct, while religious practices are acquired. If the drunk continues to progress downward, even their spirituality will be destroyed.

    Demons realize they may lose some souls from the drunken chains that they forged. So they establish a contingency plan in case the drunk ever decides to become sober. While living the drunken lifestyle, alcoholics are very open to demonic suggestion. They manipulate memory and emotions so that the drunk progressively dislikes religion. It is natural for alcoholics to begin recovery with this demonic delusion intact. It is normal for many drunks to have great difficulty with religion. Religion is the visible reminder of their guilt and rejection of God. The alcoholic's religious formation has been severely damaged and often the road to recovery begins at the crossroad where hatred and religion meet. They dislike religion because they do not have the Holy Spirit to emote the behavior they do not understand. The aversion to religion is a residual demonic influence caused by drunkenness.

If the sober alcoholic is living the spiritual life without being religious, there is the possibility that he could make spiritual progress but he is unguided and therefore open to all sorts of ungodly distractions. If he is making genuine spiritual progress without the church, the ultimate ceiling of his progress is much lower.

## Dry Drunks are Hypersensitive to the Pain of Recovery

There is a side to God the Father which God the Son did not demonstrate. God allowed illness as a consequence for sin. God the Father pronounced a lot of misfortune including sickness and death to occur as a consequence of sin. These are listed in Deuteronomy 28:15-63. In addition, God allowed blindness (2 Kings 6:18), leprosy (2 Chronicles 26:19), bowel disease (2 Chronicles 21:15) and a shriveled hand (1 Kings 13:4). God allowed two deaths through Peter's intercession (Acts 5:1-10) and he directly caused Paul to be blind (Acts 9:8). God destroyed entire nations because of their disobedience. God never promised physical healing to all Christians.

God has often used suffering (John 11:1-4, Acts 9:36-42, Galatians 4:13, 2 Corinthians 12:7-10) as a means to help mankind. Suffering has caused people to evaluate their lives and recommit it to Christ. It has prepared people for death, judgment, and eternity. It has also promoted the development of character, virtue, and grace in the alcoholic. Some alcoholics have become better people because of experiencing suffering, but no one has become a better person because of experiencing drunkenness.

Alcoholics are very aware when their body or mind is in pain. They experience the physical pain of craving, overdose, and hangovers; they experience the psychological pain of embarrassment and shame; and they experience the social pain of broken and damaged relationships. Interestingly, they do not achieve this level of awareness with their spiritual pain. Spiritual pain is generally below their perceptual threshold, but it motivates much of their behavior. They are blind to its existence, yet they daily act out its presence. Since spiritual pain is not as perceivable, it must accumulate to great proportions in order to be as perceivable as a splinter. Alcoholics would have to be in spiritual pain to such a high degree that if their heart had equal pain it would go into arrest. By the time spiritual pain has grown enough to be perceived, it is often too late for anything less than extreme measures.

Whether pain is spiritual, mental, or physical, it is a normal part of life. The drunk, dry drunk, and the sober alcoholic all experience pain. Since pain is unavoidable and a normal part of life, the only choice is to experience either the pain which leads to death or the pain which leads to life. Which hurts more, the pain of sobriety, or the sober realization that during a drunken rampage you crashed your car and killed three generations of an innocent family?

The alcoholic's sin of drunkenness merits God's punishment. Even when sobriety is joined by repentance, it does not remove the deserved punishment. All human beings reap what they sow. The alcoholic should bear these consequences in a manner pleasing to God. God knows it is better for the alcoholic to experience punishment after drunkenness. God will not "enable" the drunk.

Humbly accepting the pain of punishment has value to the recovering alcoholic because it is God's will that they be punished by Him. St. Paul was indifferent to affliction. It is better to suffer greatly during this short life than to forfeit eternal glory. At the hour of death the drunk, full of overwhelming regrets, would gladly suffer all sorts of tortures on Earth rather than lose Heaven. What worldly consolation is there for eternity in hell? When suffering is deserved, it is better to get the rightful consequence in this world, rather than in the next.

Eventually the sober alcoholic's suffering transforms from punishment to a trial. Over time, justice has been met and the sin paid for. The pain experienced takes on a new nature. Pain has a redemptive power. The suffering associated with sobriety is the daily carrying of the cross and dying in Christ, which Jesus prescribed to all on the royal road of recovery. Sobriety is a living sacrifice because every fiber of the alcoholic seems to be screaming for alcohol. Actually, when the drunk abstains, he is dying in Christ. Jesus was serious when He said we should die to ourselves and daily take up our cross. The abstinent alcoholic usually carries a very heavy cross; the dry drunk cannot bear its weight.

Interestingly, the more pain the drunk feels, the better his chances of forsaking alcohol. Unfortunately, the more pain the dry drunk feels the more likely he is to begin drinking again. He remembers that alcohol soothed his pain better than aspirin relieved his hangovers.

In years past a convicted criminal would have to run the gauntlet. As the criminal progressed through the gauntlet he would be struck. The pain was excruciating but necessary to pay for the crime and to receive freedom. The road of Christian recovery and spiritual progress is like a gauntlet. On each side of the road demons line up with weapons designed to inflict the most mortal wounds. At each step the alcoholic is hit with arrows of vice, spears of sin, and swords of guilt and shame. His spiritual life's blood is spilled as the demons assault all those who walk on this road. Only those who possess valor in the face of the enemy will achieve heroic proportions of spiritual progress.

      The dry drunk does not have the fortitude or perseverance necessary to embrace the pain associated with recovery and spiritual growth. The dry drunk must understand that the pain of recovery hurts less than the pain of relapse. He needs to accept and embrace the pain rather than avoid and flee from it. This pain is a necessary experience for all alcoholics who truly wish to progress on the road of Christian recovery. Recovering alcoholics must be counseled so that they do not mistake the pain as a sign of failure. Embracing pain is the only way to ensure sobriety. Unfortunately for dry drunks, they flee from their pain. This only increases their misery and chances of relapse. Exposing the dry drunk to the pain of recovery has as much spiritual benefit as exposing a pig to the alphabet.

# THE SACRED SCIENCE OF RECOVERY FROM ALCOHOL

### Preparation for the Reign of Jesus Christ

God has the inclination to restore and re-establish the full healing ministry to His church. The remnant of genuine faith healers and Christian counselors will exponentially increase. They will base their treatment on the power of God. Even among the non-saved the church will be established as healer while the secular healer will be put down. The healings will be a witness to non-Christian healers and cause them to accept Jesus as the Lord of their life and treatment methods. This will only be one of the many outpourings of the Holy Spirit connected with Jesus' return. God has a plan to restore mankind's spirit, soul, and body. Being the same yesterday, today, and forever, Jesus has always been the Great Physician and the Wonderful Counselor.

Most recently, even the psychologist has been displaced by the substance abuse counselor. Often the treatment manager is a non-licensed Twelve Step sponsor. The natural progression will be a full circle return to the priest, minister, reverend, or chaplain as the physician of the soul.

The Christian interested in a medical or counseling career will spend more time in prayer than in studies. They will understand that the fervent prayer of a righteous healer has much more therapeutic power than years of secular treatment. Healing is a ministry and those interested in healing will have the option to be trained in the Godly ways to heal. They will be proactive and motivate the church to pray with them. When hundreds of thousands of people pray and fast, then the lone minister who says, "Satan come out," or "Be healed," will be backed up by a multitude. The voice of the lone minister would virtually be the voice and active prayer of the whole church. God's power will manifest itself mightily.

Empowered with the gift of discernment, the authority to cast out demons, and to heal the sick, the Christian is a captain in the Army of Christ. The demonic forces will try to terrorize him. If the Christian stops attacking them, they will stop attacking him, but this is unacceptable to the Christian. This peace treaty is a pact with the devil. When a Christian is persecuted for Christ's sake, they have eternal riches and rewards.

In one day the kingdom of God will be upon many of those most in need. In the twinkling of an eye, God's glory will manifest itself and Satan will lose much.

There will be a renewing of Godly power and knowledge of Satan's previously secret plans. It is written that Satan's power is reduced as his workings become known to man. So be it.

One day all secular scientific healers will stand before the Great Physician to give an account of their practice. Despite science's attempt to market their agenda, God's mind has not been influenced. Excuses like, "I did not think it my place to counsel patients on spiritual matters," or "Spiritual counsel was outside the purview of my position," will not be well accepted by the Great Physician on Judgement Day.

## Christian Recovery

What earthly souls call recovery, angels and saints call freedom from the sin of drunkenness. It is a wonderful glorious thing when a drunk repents and begins to change his life. He begins a spiritual journey, which is majestic. This journey has its share of pain. It requires effort, grace, and wisdom. Christian recovery puts the axe to alcoholism's root, the spiritual disease.

Christian recovery is a developmental process with many milestones. The first milestone is sobriety. The second is the prevention of relapse. The third milestone, spiritual sobriety, is reached when the recovering alcoholic's first two milestones have been accomplished and alcohol related issues are diminished. As the desires for alcohol lessen, the preoccupation with matters of the flesh give way and the alcoholic can concentrate on the more sublime spiritual exercises. Only after the core Christian issues become the battle line and progress is made on these does spiritual sobriety occur. Unfortunately, as recovery progresses, so does the intensity of demonic attack. At each new milestone more diabolical obstacles appear. These obstacles will be different for each sober alcoholic, but it is guaranteed that in some form they will be there.

In Christian recovery, sins of commission and omission are reduced. St. Paul discussed this concept. Sins of commission are active sins and occur when the alcoholic does something that he should not do. For example, people should not steal, kill, give in to temptation, or get drunk, but they do. Sins of omission are passive sins and occur when the alcoholic does not do something that they should do. He begins to pray less, miss church and Twelve Step meetings, and neglects to call a pastor or sponsor when in crisis. Preventing the alcoholic from doing those necessary things that would ensure continued recovery become the demonic agenda. The demons know that sins of omission very often lead to sins of commission. It does not matter to them whether the alcoholic actively transgresses God's law or passively avoids doing good.

Putting off the old nature through abstinence is necessary but insufficient to ensure continued recovery. Christian recovery also requires putting on the new nature. Examples of putting away the old nature include cessation of drunkenness and other sins. They should shun drinking buddies and many other attachments to the world they hold dear. They should resist temptation and persevere in trials. Examples of putting on the new nature include: the development of virtue, church attendance, prayer, fasting, conversion into the image and likeness of God, conformity and union with God's will, and becoming a better spiritual bride. The alcoholic begins to embrace those things that he finds most repugnant, i.e., effort and valor in the face of adversity.

When Christian recovery is put in the context of spiritual war, with demons vying for their agenda, it is reassuring to know that Jesus is the Great Physician and Wonderful Counselor.

## Intervention of Grace

God's healing grace can cure alcoholism. Just as Jesus told the paralytic to get up and walk; made the blind see and the deaf hear; He heals alcoholics. Not only does the progression of the disease halt, but it is pulled out at the roots. The sober alcoholic is never healed of alcoholism except in the case of divine intervention. No amount of medical treatment, counseling, or Twelve Step attendance can cure alcoholism. These mortal attempts can only promote recovery. Alcoholics often interpret prolonged abstinence to mean God healed them. It is very dangerous for alcoholics to think of themselves as healed because this can cause relapse. Usually, it is the disease's "stinking thinking" which tricks the alcoholic into believing he is healed. Since the drunk has to deal with recovery, not healing, their prognosis depends a lot on their spiritual condition and the disease's degree of progression. A general guideline is that it takes more faith and power to restore an amputated leg than to cure a toothache. Another guideline is that a chronic illness takes more power to heal than an acute illness. This means that it takes more faith to help the alcoholic of 20 years who drinks a fifth of whiskey per day than it does to help the alcoholic of 5 years. Recovery is generally more difficult for the person who during his life was in worse condition. Nevertheless, there may be an immediate miraculous healing of a severe chronic alcoholic, while at other times there may be a gradual partial healing. It is a divine mystery why these patterns occur.

God's model of healing and disease has not changed since He is the same yesterday, today, and forever. He has said, "I the Lord do not change." (Malachi 3:6). He also declared in Deuteronomy 32:39, "...I put to death and I bring to life, I have wounded and I heal..." He causes illness as punishment and a rebuke (2 Chronicles 26:18-21, Deuteronomy 28:15-68) and cures illness when people obey Him (Exodus 23:25). God has used a variety of methods for healing. He has used the statue of a bronze serpent (Numbers 21:8), mud (John 9:6-7), spit (Mark 7:33), the casting out of demons (Mark 1:25-26), oil (James 5:14), the playing of a musical instrument (1 Samuel 16:23), sorrow (2 Corinthians 7:10), figs (2 Kings 20:7), St. Peter's shadow (Acts 5:14-16), and water (2 Kings 5:14). Jesus' ministry also included the practice of medicine. He cured blindness (Matthew 9:28-30; 12:22, Mark 10:51-52), fever (Luke 4:38-39), deafness and muteness (Mark 7:32-35), replaced an amputated ear (Luke 22:50-51), leprosy (Luke 5:12-13; Mark 1:40-42), hemorrhages (Matthew 9:20-22), the lame and crippled (Matthew 15:30-31), paralytics (Matthew 9:2-7), a withered hand (Matthew 12:9-13), cast out demons (Matthew 8:31-32, Mark 1:23-26), and cured what scientists call epilepsy (Mark 9:25-27). He also restored life to the dead (John 11:38-44). Jesus delegated his power and authority to his followers (Luke 9:1-2, 10:19, Matthew 10:1). The apostles manifested that power and authority given to them. In Jesus' name, they cast out devils (Acts 8:7), cured fever (Acts 28:8-9), and cripples (Acts 14:8-10, Acts 3:6-9). St. Paul raised a man from the dead (Acts 20:9-12). God gave His church great power and authority over illness.

The Great Physician continues to heal through many different methods. Sometimes He directly administers healing without human intervention. In order to accomplish this He has established biological mechanisms that prevent illness as well as automatically fight it. He also directly empowers the will, renews the mind, and heals the emotions. He directly administers His healing to the spirit, mind, and body of all human beings, even to the non-Christians. Sometimes He elects not to intervene and allows an illness to continue uninterrupted until death. At other times He heals through the intervention of a scientific healer or minister.

There are no set rules for the order of recovery, only guidelines. In fact, as a guideline, God will orchestrate the alcoholic's healing in the way most beneficial to them. Recovery is like a horse race. At the start horse A takes the lead. Soon, horse B has a burst of speed and takes the lead only fading in the long run to have horse C eventually take the lead. Spiritual, mental, and physical recovery are like horses A, B, and C. It matters little which component initiates or temporarily dominates the process, as long as the spiritual component is engaged.

It is imperative that the alcoholic solicits God's help and receives His favor. The Holy Spirit gives the Christian alcoholic spiritual gifts to persevere in his recovery. These are gifts he gives to his children, not the children of the world. With a surgeon's skill, the Holy Spirit cuts out hindrances, obstacles, and barriers, which impede spiritual progress and Christian recovery. There is hardly a drunken soul who can begin recovery, except by God's grace. It can transform a drunk to a saint. It has happened before and can happen again.

Recovery has limits. Physical recovery is the first component to reach its limit. After detoxification and a short adjustment period the sober alcoholic's body has reached its recovery potential. In some cases there are permanent impediments which require the alcoholic to learn acceptance. In physical recovery the healing process is virtually done by God, since sobriety is the only necessary human action. Medical treatment can help during detoxification. If God decides not to remove or lessen the desire to drink, the use of antabuse may be inspired. Even though the spiritual body is more important than the physical body, Christian bodies are members of Christ, temples of the Holy Spirit and sacred. Because the physical body holds this exalted position in God's eyes, it is prudent to protect it from the damage caused by drunkenness. The Christian in recovery who relapses is negligent in his responsibility to maintain the temple of the Holy Spirit.

The ceiling for psychological recovery is much higher than it is for physical recovery. It requires much more cooperation with God's grace. The alcoholic can improve his soul by studying the literature on alcoholism and improve his emotions by Christian counseling. His mind can be renewed and his will purified as well as empowered.

Spiritual recovery is without ceiling. They can improve spiritually by continuous conversion, prayer, Bible reading, and church attendance. The sober alcoholic can progress from glory to glory. Each time they make spiritual progress the ceiling actually raises. Who could ever predict that a spiritual awakening could steal an alcoholic from the demon's claws and nurture them to become holy and acceptable to God.

Often, Christian recovery begins at an unobservable level. Just as an illness can exist in an asymptomatic state so can the early stages of recovery. To the casual observer the alcoholic may still appear to be a drunk. They drink daily, act psychotic, have blackouts and continuous hangovers. During the drunk's deepest, darkest, most demonic moments, God's grace spared his life from suicide, overdose, or fatal accident to allow for future repentance. The very first sign of healing grace is the drunk's half-honest desire to change. Then God's grace fills the soul with hidden virtues to make a spiritual decision: to amend his life and stop the sin of drunkenness. After repentance, grace continues to operate in the recovering alcoholic to reactivate his conscience, which alcohol has seared. Sobriety is only the beginning, not the end of the operation of grace. Up to this point God's grace had provided only the remedial work necessary to allow them to begin their ascent to spiritual perfection. This remedial work is a wonderful example of a loving Father's forgiveness for vile sins committed against Him. It changes the course of the alcoholic's soul from eternal hell to God's presence, and he begins to brush off the dust and ash of hell.

At times, the recovering alcoholic will receive so much grace that his spiritual exercises soar to new heights and appear almost superhuman. If this time of grace is not properly managed the recovering alcoholic, who has great zeal, may fail to notice when the grace for these extraordinary acts is withdrawn. The alcoholic can easily mistake personal resolve for God's will. They continue the extraordinary practices on their own strength, without the corresponding internal grace. This will only bring disappointment and frustration and could possibly trigger a relapse. The recovering alcoholic must be empowered by God to pursue spiritual progress and then proceed by his own free will.

## Spiritual Exercises for Spiritual Warfare

God has stated that exercise for the body is good, but much less important than spiritual exercise. In terms of eternity the physical body is here today, gone tomorrow. Some quadriplegics go to heaven in an incorrupt immortal body, while some athletes go to hell.

## Important Reasons For Combining Religion With Spirituality

Many sober alcoholics have great difficulty when they try to reestablish themselves in the church. They certainly do not experience serenity. This is normal, not the exception. Being in church is an awesome holy experience and until recently the drunk was destined for hell. It is truly culture shock.

The alcoholic's sin does not exclude them from going to church. They can go to church hung over every Sunday just as long as they always go. Unfortunately, the other people at church are also working out their own salvation. Each comes complete with his own unique complex of sin and imperfections. Some may be involved in very grave sin and thus be spiritually dead. For example, the unrepentant adulterer is in worse condition than the humble sober alcoholic is.

The church is a visible sign of God's dominion, but many recovering alcoholics do not see this. Their gaze about church is the opposite of euphoric recall. As a drunk, they looked at the living church with their dead eyes and determined it dead. But it was they who were dead, not the church. Do not expect the living church to be perceived alive by the dead. In order to understand that the church is alive, the alcoholic must be born again. After their spiritual awakening, they must reevaluate for themselves if the church is dead or alive. God will allow those who truly seek Him to see the church's internal spiritual life.

Alcoholics Anonymous does not do what church does because it is not church. Only church can do what church is intended to do. When alcoholics initially begin recovery they often have more in common with other alcoholics than with the general Christian population. There is a time in their recovery when they need the fellowship of other recovering alcoholics. If the recovering alcoholic is only concerned about sobriety then Alcoholics Anonymous is sufficient, but the Christian church offers direction and grace that Alcoholics Anonymous does not claim to give. Alcoholics Anonymous by itself can only take the recovering alcoholic so far. Even Alcoholics Anonymous attendance with the higher power as the Holy Trinity is not as beneficial as regular church attendance. There comes a time in the Christian alcoholic's recovery when they must return to church. Since recently sober alcoholics are spiritual babies, how can their Christian formation be properly shaped if not exposed to the role model of the more mature Christian? They need to fellowship with strong, mature Christians, many of whom never had a drinking problem. Alcoholics Anonymous attendance, with a Christian sponsor, combined with regular church attendance is the royal road for most recovering alcoholics.

Demons do not want the alcoholic in church because it is much easier for them to manipulate an alcoholic not nurtured by the church. Generally a predator does not attack the strong, healthy animal in the herd, but searches for an isolated, weakened victim. Remember that Satan roams around like a lion looking for someone to devour. He will chew up and spit out the sober alcoholic who does not go to church. Only the demons benefit from the recovering alcoholic avoiding church. Drunkenness promotes the demonic agenda because the drunk is not present in his proper state, at church to fill the unique place made especially for him by Providence.

God would like all recovering Christian alcoholics to have a healthy balance between spirituality and religion. They should have the desirable traits of both, without the faults of either. As light is to a fire, religion is to spirituality. They are more than two sides of the same coin. Religion and spirituality are the same thing in different form, just like water and steam.

The spiritual and religious were meant to coexist simultaneously in order that grace may abound. The integration of spirituality and religion is God's will and therefore a necessary milestone in the recovery of the Christian alcoholic. Spirituality and religion must be united in the soul of the recovering alcoholic.

Ideal Christian recovery includes religious and spiritual activities. Certain internal spiritual dispositions cannot be acquired without the habitual practice of corresponding religious acts. This is because the Christian church is not part of the world but rather a material manifestation of the spiritual realm. God highly values the practices of religion like Bible study, prayer, and fasting, as well as the spiritual dispositions like patience, mercy, love, hope, etc. Without the exterior practices of religion the internal spiritual dispositions are weakened and are soon defeated by the wear and tear of the enemy. The person who has a genuine internal spirituality which manifests itself in reasonable religious practices has gone far on the road of Christian recovery and made much spiritual progress.

Many people try to make a distinction between religion and spirituality when there is much more in common between them than different. Two men may be of different races, heights, weights, and statures, yet they are both fully men. There is more in common between them than different. This issue between spirituality versus religion, as if the two were competing ways of life, is as old as Cain and Abel, and has been fully explained by all the major religions. Mankind has tried to separate the two as if it were possible to get a pound of flesh without blood.

The spiritual person without religion and the religious person without spirituality are both handicapped and need to be healed. A break on the bridge that connects spirituality and religion hinders recovery whichever side is preferred.

**The Value of Bible Reading for Recovery**

The Jews revered the Old Testament. They considered the Bible so holy that they would not touch it with their hands. They respected the Bible in ways many Christian do not understand. Today, Bibles are so common that people throw the Bible around, sit on it, use it to save a seat at church, and scribble notes in it. If an ancient Jew ever treated their Sacred Scripture that way they would probably have been executed.

Historically, only the rich could afford to purchase a handwritten Bible. Besides, most of the early church members could not read. The Gospel was proclaimed verbally, through artwork like stained glass windows, oil paintings, or statues. Times have certainly changed. Nowadays many of the Christian community can read.

God grants grace to the person who reads the Bible. The reader learns what God likes and how God responds to situations. God's thought patterns become imprinted on the reader.

There are several things the recovering alcoholic must consider when inspired to be devoted to God through study of His holy word. There are many translations of the Bible and not every version is appropriate. An older translation might say, "How art thou?" while a contemporary version might say, "How are you?" Even within contemporary Bibles some translations are written on the Ph.D. level while others can be read by a high school student. If a good intentioned recovering alcoholic with poor reading skills selected an archaic translation they might be discouraged from reading it.

Once the proper translation is selected, there are many different systems for reading the Bible. There is some value in reading the Bible for historical reference or to examine the structure of a poem, but any value derived from these activities is carnal, not spiritual. It is a good thing to read the entire Bible annually. When the entire Bible is read, the reader is confronted with all that God has revealed to man. If they read only selected verses they may unconsciously avoid important passages. If reading the entire Bible is too overwhelming, they should try to read the entire New Testament each year. Most recovering alcoholics are not spiritually mature enough to undertake the monumental task of reading so much annually. God understands man's weakness. It takes time to develop a system of scripture reading, which takes into account God's will for you. Read what you can, in God's grace, and do not feel guilty. Many of those who read the entire Bible annually race through it and acquire less grace than the one who reads a little, within their ability, and reads it prayerfully and devoutly.

If reading only a little bit is the best you can do, consider reading all the verses which discuss drunkenness. Unfortunately, all this information is buried deep in often neglected books of the Bible. Therefore, sections of the Bible that deal with drunkenness are clearly presented here. Replication has been kept to a minimum.

Noah, a man of the soil, proceeded to plant a vineyard. When he drank some of its wine, he became drunk and lay uncovered inside his tent (Genesis 9:21).

Let's get our father to drink wine and then lie with him and preserve our family line through our father (Genesis 19:32).

You and your sons are not to drink wine or other fermented drink when ever you go into the Tent of Meeting, or you will die (Leviticus 10:9).

If a man or woman wants to make a special vow, a vow of separation to the Lord as a Nazarite, he must abstain from wine and other fermented drink and must not drink vinegar made from wine or from other fermented drink (Numbers 6:3).

They shall say to the elders, "This son of ours is stubborn and rebellious. He will not obey us. He is a profligate and a drunkard." Then all the men of his town shall stone him to death. You must purge the evil from among you (Deuteronomy 21:20-21).

Wine is a mocker and beer a brawler; whoever is led astray by them is not wise (Proverbs 20:1).

Do not join those who drink too much wine or gorge themselves on meat, for drunkards and gluttons become poor, and drowsiness clothes them in rags (Proverbs 23:21).

Like a thornbush in a drunkard's hand is a proverb in the mouth of a fool (Proverbs 26:9).

Woe to those who rise early in the morning to run after their drinks, who stay up late at night till they are inflamed with wine (Isaiah 5:11).

Woe to those who are heroes at drinking wine and champions at mixing drinks... (Isaiah 5:22).

The Lord has poured into them a spirit of dizziness...as a drunkard staggers around in his vomit (Isaiah 19:14).

He will be a joy and delight to you, and many will rejoice because of his birth, for he will be great in the sight of the Lord.

He is never to take wine or other fermented drink, and he will be filled with the Holy Spirit even from birth (Luke 1:14-15).

Let us behave decently, as in the daytime, not in orgies and drunkenness, not in sexual immorality and debauchery, not in dissension and jealousy. Rather clothe yourselves with the Lord Jesus Christ, and do not think about how to gratify the desires of the sinful nature (Romans 13:13-14).

But now I am writing you that you must not associate with anyone who calls himself a brother but is sexually immoral or greedy, an idolater or a slanderer, a drunkard or a swindler. With such a man do not even eat (1 Corinthians 5:11).

Do not be deceived: Neither the sexually immoral nor idolaters nor adulterers nor male prostitutes nor homosexual offenders nor thieves nor the greedy nor drunkards nor slanders nor swindlers will inherit the kingdom of God (1 Corinthians 6:9-10).

The acts of the sinful nature are obvious: sexual immorality, impurity and debauchery; idolatry and witchcraft; hatred, discord, jealousy, fits of rage, self ambition, dissensions, factions and envy; drunkenness, orgies and the like. I warn you, as I did before, that those who live like this will not inherit the kingdom of God (Galatians 5:19-21).

Do not get drunk on wine, which leads to debauchery. Instead, be filled with the Spirit (Ephesians 5:18).

The end of all things is near. Therefore be clear minded and self controlled so that you can pray (1 Peter 4:7).

Be self-controlled and alert. Your enemy the devil prowls around like a roaring lion looking for someone to devour (1 Peter 5:8).

**Types of Prayer Important to Alcoholics**

In the Old Testament, a person serious about prayer would lay on the ground. Tradition has taught that kneeling is an appropriate position. Other body positions are less beneficial because they hinder communion with God. In addition to the position of the body when in prayer, the location is also important. Solitude and silence should be the rule, not the exception.

Prayer is spiritual warfare. It hinders demonic activity. Often it is not only preparing for a future battle, but it is the actual battle. The demons do not want Christian alcoholics to pray. Demons are very skilled in activating both internal and external obstacles to prevent an alcoholic from praying. Two reasons demons hate and fear prayer so much is because it transforms the Christian alcoholic into God's image and those devout in prayer can actually take authority over the demons. The continual, fervent prayer of a righteous person causes them great difficulty in accomplishing their diabolical agenda. Even non-fervent sporadic prayer from a fallen Christian disturbs them.

Early morning prayer is a way to dedicate the day to God and His care. Morning prayer requires more effort and demonstrates a much more serious commitment to God and sobriety. For the newly sober alcoholic, getting up early to pray is very difficult. The sleep patterns of the drunk were under demonic influence for years. God understands the alcoholic's struggle with alcohol better than anyone does. It is an unnecessary burden to feel guilty when not praying in the early morning. Simply pray as soon as you can. Just because the majority of mature Christians rise up early to pray does not mean that the newly sober alcoholic should live up to those standards. Eventually, as you mature, getting up early to pray will become as natural as breathing. If there is ever a time or place when you experience chronic misery or severe temptation, then by all means pray early in the morning. It has been said that the early bird catches the worm and in the same way, the alcoholic who gets up early to pray catches God's special attention.

Many recovering Christian alcoholics think they are doing a great feat when they pray five minutes per day. This is truly good, but in reality it is the least they could do. Anyone can pray inconsistently, erratically, and selfishly, but successful prayer requires enough time to truly communicate with God. To bear your soul and hear from God requires more than occasional prayer. It requires lengthy, daily prayer. The Christian alcoholic in recovery must become a person devoted to prayer. Even when doing daily chores, there can be an unbroken and continuous wordless communication in the soul. Prayer warriors have developed the practice of continual prayer.

There once was a man in the habit of praying on his knees at church for about two hours every day. One day a person commended him about the length of time he devoted to prayer. In response he said that he actually only prayed for a few minutes each day because it took him over an hour to get to the internal state from which he could pop in and out of genuine prayer for brief moments. This is the understanding of a general in the army of prayer warriors. For those recently converted from drunkenness, just know that if you are on your knees praying for two hours, even if your mind wanders from prayer, so long as you put your attention back to prayer when you notice it wandered, your two hours count. Alcoholics should beg God to provide grace for their continued sobriety and be sure to thank Him for each day they remain sober. Jesus instructed Christians to watch and pray so that they would not fall into temptation (Matthew 26:41). Prayer reduces and prevents anxiety (Philippians 4:6) and God protects those who pray (Ezra 8:23). God will always provide guideposts to those traveling on the road of spiritual progress. Pray that you perceive and follow those guideposts.

Prayers done in the form of vain repetition are not prayers according to God's will. A parrot could be taught to recite the Lord's Prayer but of what spiritual value is it? Many humans recite this prayer with little more value than a parrot. They mindlessly recite the words without focus of mind or heartfelt sentiment while meditating on daily events or worse, on sin. Alcoholics must develop their ability to concentrate during prayer. It is not the amount of words uttered, but their quality. For the Lord's Prayer to be a fervent prayer with much power, the thirty second rendition is often inadequate. The short rendition is a valid prayer, especially for the large congregation, but the longer, more communicative rendition has more recovery value. With a little practice, this prayer can be transformed into a one hour rendition.

Praying the Lord's Prayer at each Twelve Step meeting is certainly spiritually correct and of benefit to everyone regardless of what spiritual level those participating are at. It is the most perfect prayer known since God Himself instructed His apostles to pray this prayer. It is a wonderful testimony to the all-pervasive providence of God that this prayer is regularly included in a chemical dependency treatment program.

Corporate prayer is very important since when two or three are gathered in Jesus' name there is much power. God may act on the fervent prayer of a Twelve Step group that is petitioning Him to help someone. Remember, Jesus said, "If you believe, you will receive whatever you ask for in prayer." (Matthew 21:22). In the cases when God causes illness for chastisement, the fervent prayer of a righteous healer will not heal the ill person unless their prayers change the mind of God. The point is that all healing has to do with God's will, not the will of the healer or the person seeking healing. When people pray they often pray according to their own will. The Wonderful Counselor prescribes that alcoholics pray in the spirit, with the spirit, and through the spirit, but human nature often interferes with the complete surrender of the will in prayer.

Alcoholics in recovery need to learn and practice all the various forms of prayer. At the minimum, their prayer life should consist of intercessory prayer, prayers of repentance and mercy, and authoritative prayer.

## Intercessory Prayer

Most recovering alcoholics pray for themselves more often than they pray for others. When they pray for their own needs they are petitioning God to grant a personal request. It is God's will that alcoholics pray for themselves. Personal prayer is important because it helps the alcoholic to be filled with the Holy Spirit and resist temptation. Unfortunately, most drunks actually pray that God would enable them and this practice does not go away with the start of sobriety.

When the alcoholic prays for himself it is good, but when he prays for others, the prayer becomes intercessory prayer. Intercessory prayer requires much more stamina than personal prayer because it is not selfishly motivated. By praying for another the alcoholic takes the focus off himself. This is a great feat for the self centered alcoholic. Christian alcoholics in recovery need to practice interceding for those God brings into their sphere of awareness, whether physically or in thought. It is a very difficult task for a Christian to intercede for an enemy but Jesus requires it (Matthew 5:44). When the recovering Christian prays for the needs of another they are granted a special healing grace. This grace not only helps the person for whom they pray; it also helps the intercessor stay sober.

There is also another way intercessory prayer can help the alcoholic. Without the intercessory prayer of mature Christians, the drunk may not even have enough conscience to be able to hit bottom. Without intercessory prayer, the drunk may never muster enough humility to ask for needed help. Intercessory prayer can make them want sobriety.

Intercessors function as beacons of light in their dark and depraved world. Many Christians would be happy to intercede for the drunk. The drunk should let their family and friends know their need for prayer. Drunks do not have to admit to God, themselves, or the person they are asking for prayer, that they are alcoholics, powerless, or unable to manage their lives. They just have to communicate that they are having a problem with drinking and would like them to ask God to help them stop. The more honest they are about their powerlessness or inability to manage their life, the better able the person can intercede for them, but the point is that even a drunk can ask for prayer. Drunks should continuously and constantly ask as many Christians as possible to pray for them.

## Prayers of Repentance and Mercy

The drunk's prayers are not guaranteed to incline God to hear, but God does hear the prayers of those who are truly repentant; this includes the sincere penitent alcoholic. God will receive a prayer of repentance, no matter how much their drunken behavior offended Him. The only thing that prevents the drunk from crying out to God for healing and mercy is a lack of desire for such salvation. If they could only beg for God's mercy they may be spared eternal damnation. God will usually help whoever asks Him, especially if asked in Jesus' name. If they truly want to stop drinking they will probably even pray for God's help while falling down drunk.

Prayers of repentance require more than simply confessing sin. Self examination, with the putting aside of the psychological defense mechanisms, must be accomplished. This is not an easy task since it is natural to blame someone else, forget, or rationalize a sinful behavior. Nevertheless, the alcoholic must be honest with himself and God. This process is very painful, but once accomplished it brings healing, cleansing, and restoration with God. Hardly a soul makes it even one day without committing a sin. Therefore prayers of repentance should be commonly practiced.

## Authoritative Prayer

Authoritative prayer is much different than all other forms of prayer. Prayers of repentance, praise, worship, thanksgiving, and even intercession are prayers which are lifted up to God. Authoritative prayer travels downward. The person using authoritative prayer calls down God's power and commands supernatural spiritual acts on persons, places, things, or situations, as needed for the advancement of God's Kingdom. In authoritative prayer God's power and authority make a supernatural act occur.

Jesus told his apostles if they had faith they could speak to the mountain and it would be moved into the sea. Jesus did not advise them to petition God to move the mountain. He told them to authoritatively command it to move. All prayer is warfare but the distinction that prayer is toward God and warfare toward the devil needs to be understood. To illustrate, at church a baby was crying and screaming while its mother was trying to calm it. The baby was crying for about thirty minutes. As the service began, a member of the congregation placed his hand on the crying child's head and said, "God's peace be with you, little one." Instantly, the baby stopped crying and began to coo. That was authoritative prayer. God's will was called down.

Inexperienced intercessors pray for physical healing and often add, "if it is Your will, God." When someone prays, "if it is Your will," they are not praying the prayer of faith, but rather a prayer of either hope or disbelief. Some literally beg the illness to leave instead of commanding it to go. The prayer warrior prays with authority, in the form of a command, and does not beg the illness to leave. He boldly proclaims, in Jesus' name, for the illness to leave.

The most important thing to remember about prayer is that all alcoholics should spend less time studying and talking about prayer, and pray always and about everything.

**Why Fasting is Especially Important to Alcoholics**

Fasting is a very important part of the alcoholic's recovery provided it is done for the right reasons. Jesus taught that the person fasting should not make the spiritual exercise public knowledge. Instead they must try to conceal their fasting. When a person fasts for worldly recognition, that is all they receive. They have substituted spiritual for temporal rewards.

Nevertheless, all things being equal, a spiritual fast is superior to a dietary fast. Many diet but are not fasting. This is not to detract from the value of dietary fasting. At the physiological level dietary fasting has great value. It rids the body of toxins, waste, and diseased tissue. It gives the digestive system a rest. The energy used for digestion is redirected. Since the brain and soul are linked, the soul residually benefits from non-spiritual fasting. Concentration, perception, etc., improve with dieting. Nevertheless, there are absolutely no spiritual benefits from dietary fasting.

Spiritual fasting is much more than merely abstaining from food. True fasting requires dedication of the fast to God. Certainly the person fasting should avoid sin. Proper spiritual fasting involves prayer. When the apostles could not cast out a demon Jesus told them that this kind of demon could only be cast out by prayer and fasting. Not prayer alone. Not fasting alone. Many people pray but neglect to fast.

God correctly perceives the heart of the person fasting. He knows the difference between spiritual fasting and dietary fasting. When true spiritual fasting occurs, it is an act of faith, with the intent to worship, and includes prayer. God responds quickly and powerfully to genuine fasting. This is a wonderful spiritual discipline that continually perfects the practitioner. It increases grace and diminishes the sin nature. Fasting also keeps the body in subjection to the spirit.

Fasting is important for the spiritual growth of all Christians, but there are also some specific benefits for Christian alcoholics. Since drunkenness is gluttony and fasting is the opposite of gluttony, it restores exactly that which was destroyed by drunkenness. Fasting puts an end to the pathological hunger drive. It strengthens the recovering alcoholic's resolve to remain sober and reduces the temptation to drink.

For drunken alcoholics who cannot fast from food, it would be beneficial if they could muster the fortitude to offer God a partial fast. Some eat only one meal a day; others eat only bread or fruit juice. Others abstain from meat. For the Christian alcoholic in recovery the medium to be fasted would not be food, but alcohol. It would not be done with the intention to permanently give up alcohol. It would be done only to fast. The drunk who can fast under a vow, to make the old time pledge, is truly blessed. When a person fasts they give up something they have a right to have: food. God is only asking that the drunk give up a sin that they should hate. God knows if it is more difficult for one person to give up alcohol than it is for another to give up food. When drunks surrender their right to drink, they crucify their flesh and die to sin.

A quick and sure way for alcoholics to quickly progress in their recovery is to fast and offer the consequent pain as a living sacrifice. This fast would be an act of contrition, offered to God for the remission of due punishment for sin. By fasting from alcohol, the recovering alcoholic is merely doing the least he should do. In order to make unbelievable spiritual progress he must fast from alcohol and food.

It just makes good sense to everyone except the person with the drinking problem that moderate drinking is not an option for them. The alcoholic who considers drinking is like the man who flirts with an adulteress. Sooner or later he is doomed. It is much easier for the alcoholic to practice the virtue of abstinence than temperance; to avoid drinking altogether, than to tempt God.

The newly sober alcoholic is generally limited to spiritual milk, but spiritual milk is much better than worldly beer, liquor, or wine. Sober alcoholics do not need spiritual junk food; they need good solid spiritual food in order to progress spiritually. Solid spiritual food will help them resist temptation and decrease their lust for alcohol. They will drink living water and feed on spiritual food.

**Improve Recovery by the Examination of the Conscience**

A good examination of conscience is necessary for the alcoholic's spiritual recovery. It gives them an opportunity to become aware of and acknowledge their sins, ask God's forgiveness, and renew their resolve to resist temptation. They must not only note the wrong things they did, but also the things they failed to do as well as the motives behind their actions.

Examination of conscience allows alcoholics an opportunity to see themselves as God sees them. This gets them in touch with the reality they have spent years denying and avoiding. This is important because as they recover they have a distorted view of themselves. Family and friends also have a distorted view of them.

Upon rising, the alcoholic should resolve to avoid the sin of drunkenness. Throughout the day they should review their compliance with this resolution and note when they dwelled on temptation. The alcoholic should determine the things that could trigger a relapse and resolve to avoid them. As many times as they experience weakness, they should renew their resolution.

Most chronic drunks have destroyed their conscience. In order to reinstate the conscience, alcoholics should expose themselves to God's objective morality by prayer, church attendance, and reading the Holy Bible.

## Christian Meditation

The Apostle Paul exhorted Christians to think about whatever is true, noble, right, pure, lovely, admirable, excellent, and praiseworthy (Philippians 4:8). He also recommended that Christians should set their minds on things that are above, not on things that are on earth (Colossians 3:2). This is accomplished by several methods. Closing the eyes and focusing awareness on an object or phrase are some of the more common methods.

A Christian can meditate on an object, but it must steer the mind toward God. This means that a Christian cannot meditate on a secular object like a tree, or a blasphemous object like an occult symbol. Meditation on an object may work well for millions, but in some cases it triggers a desire to drink. In these cases, the recovering alcoholic would best practice meditation on a holy thought or prayer. Meditation on the short prayer, "Jesus have mercy on me, a sinner," has great value toward recovery. Meditation on the loss of heaven and the pains of hell could be a deterrent to relapse. The Christian's choice of phrases is also limited to those that are edifying. Whichever method is used, the goal is union with God. Therefore, methods that cause disunion are prohibited.

The reason that Christian alcoholics cannot hear God's voice is because their internal dialogue is too loud. This internal dialogue consists of daily events, stress, memories, and sinful thoughts. In order to hear God's voice the volume of the noise needs to be lowered. In meditation, the mind is emptied, not of knowledge or God's Holy Spirit, but all worldly noise. It is the purposeful, willful act of not perceiving external or internal sensory stimuli. Meditation quiets the alcoholic's inner dialogue. The mind needs to be free from distractions, passions, and plans. Christian meditation prevents anxiety. A tranquil mind gives life to the body (Proverbs 14:30). It creates a quietness of mind, and this internal silence promotes recovery.

Although the process of Christian and occult meditation is identical, the latter attracts demons. Christian meditation can be differentiated from its demonic counterpart by its content, context, and ultimate goal. Occult meditation does not promote union with God as its ultimate goal. Instead, its goal is oneness with the dead, impersonal universe. Meditation cannot be called Christian merely because it is practiced by a Christian, any more than psychological counseling can be called Christian merely because it is practiced by a Christian.

# The Spiritually Sober Alcoholic

## Understanding How to Truly Forgive

If alcoholics confess their sins, God is faithful and just and will forgive their sins and purify them from all unrighteousness (1 John 1:9). "Therefore, there is now no condemnation for those who are in Christ Jesus... " (Romans 8:1). The application of forgiveness can be repeated (Matthew 18:21-22). In Luke 17:3-4 Jesus said, "...If your brother sins, rebuke him, and if he repents, forgive him. If he sins against you seven times in a day, and seven times comes back to you and says, 'I repent,' forgive him."

Another important milestone on the road to Christian recovery is to receive God's forgiveness. There are several conditions that must be met in order to get His forgiveness. This means that sin is forgiven only when the proper instruments of forgiveness are applied. Impediments to God's forgiveness are the cause of more relapses than any other action.

Receiving God's forgiveness depends on the confession of the alcoholic's own sins. Confession is more than an apology. It includes repentance and a firm resolution to amend your life. All sin must be confessed to God, but the decision to confess a sin to another person must be made with discernment and prudence. Sometimes confession to the one sinned against is not God's will. Recovering alcoholics have an unnatural propensity to expiate their guilt by confessing their offenses. They confuse their unconscious motive for guilt reduction with some more noble reason. Just because confession is cathartic is no reason to further damage the one already sinned against. The confession may cause more hurt than healing; especially if the person sinned against was unaware of the sin. If the confession would elicit anger, hatred, or revenge, it is best not to confess to them. How many alcoholics with less than a year in recovery have tried to make amends with their spouse by admitting adultery and lost the love of their life forever? Only confession to God is required. Confess it to God and sin no more. Conversely, many sinners would rather only confess to God because they correctly perceive retribution instead of mercy, grace, and forgiveness. At other times it is God's will that the alcoholic confess not only to Him, but also to the person sinned against. This is the case when the offended person knows about the sin committed against them. The alcoholic's confession may be the only way the offended person can be moved to forgive. If you were brought up in a church that practices sacramental confession, as quickly as possible, go!

During the course of the drunken alcoholic's life there are many people who have offended him. This is superceded only by the number of people he has offended. The alcoholic must be forgiven as well as forgive others. Matthew 6:14-15 teaches that God's forgiveness is blocked when the sinner refuses to forgive those who have sinned against them. Forgive us our sins as we forgive those who sin against us, is a biblical principle for healing the soul. Therefore, if the Christian alcoholic is sorry for his sin and promises not to do it anymore, but holds others accountable, God's forgiveness is blocked. God will hold them accountable since they are holding other sinners accountable. The parable of the unmerciful servant (Matthew 18:21-35) illustrates this. A man was forgiven a great debt. Although he was forgiven a great debt, he refused to forgive a small debt owed to him. The parable ended with this evil man's original debt being reinstated. How can one expect God's forgiveness unless they have forgiven others? God wants sinners to forgive those who have sinned against them because it releases them from their own hurt which would otherwise ferment in their soul, boil over, and transform into sinful behavior. The result of forgiving others is a blessing on the person forgiven as well as for the one who forgives. God wants Christians to be as generous in forgiving others as He is in forgiving man (Ephesians 4:32). It is more than God's desire for mankind to forgive each other, it is a mandate (Colossians 3:13). We actually commit a sin when we refuse to forgive because the refusal is opposing God's will.

Another obstacle that blocks forgiveness and hinders recovery is when a sinner does not forgive himself. Often it is difficult for the alcoholic to forgive himself because he projects his fault on to others, and therefore does not experience any fault. In addition, drunkenness alters the drunk's perception of time. The past is relived daily, the present is escaped from, and the future does not exist. They compulsively relive long forgotten events. They obsessively repeat the dialogue and focus on vengeful outcomes. Because they cannot let go, the anger and hurt of past events are relived with their full emotional impact. They constantly reopen old wounds and respond to the memory as if it just happened. This causes them to fixate at an early stage in their recovery. When an alcoholic takes the proper steps to receive God's forgiveness but does not experience it, they are playing God, and that is what original sin is all about. When a person forgives himself it is truly a wonderful thing, not only are they the forgiven but they are also the forgiver.

The alcoholic's "stinking thinking" creates a thought process which prevents him from experiencing God's forgiveness. While it is true that all mankind is guilty of this, its per capita occurrence is exponentially higher among alcoholics. They falsely accuse God for their life's problems rather than see their own responsibility. They misdirect their anger toward God, hold a grudge against Him, and believe He sinned against them. To illustrate, a drunk was angry with God because his parents died. For thirty years he held this grudge.

He did not pray or go to church. This man angrily and willfully separated himself from God because he judged God and determined that God should have allowed his parents to live. In this case it was not God who needed to be forgiven, but a delusional thought process which needed to be healed. It would be a sin for a sponsor to counsel this alcoholic to forgive God because he would be bearing false witness against God. The sponsor would be reinforcing the alcoholic's delusional thought process. In fact, there is no sin to be forgiven because God does not sin. God is all good and deserves all our love. He is above all reproach.

## The Acquisition of Virtue

Virtue can be acquired through natural and/or supernatural methods. Strict discipline develops natural virtues. This type of virtue only comes to those who diligently and persistently exert great effort. It does not come to the lazy or insincere. Natural virtue places its possessor far above ordinary man. Natural virtue is attainable by the godless. The drunk can develop natural virtue, but not virtue that is infused by God's grace.

The Christian possesses both natural and supernatural virtue. Supernatural virtue is infused by God and not only complements natural virtue, but also transcends it. Infused virtue is directly imprinted into man's soul by God's grace. It operates independent of effort. The infusion process stops when the alcoholic becomes drunk because friendship with God is broken. Therefore, drunkenness will destroy infused virtue but only damage natural virtue. This is true because natural virtue is within the nature of man, but infused virtue is a gift from God's good grace.

It has been said of certain people that they are virtuous. This does not necessarily mean that they are good Christians.

The murderer who patiently waits for his victim may practice patience to the highest degree but it could not be said that the murderer was a virtuous man. The drunk may prudently arrange his environment to get drunk, but prudence was misapplied toward dysfunctional ends. Virtuous acts are morally neutral and can be used for good or evil ends. Therefore, virtuous acts do not make a person virtuous. Only when acts are motivated by the love of God, obedience to God, or love for others are they truly virtuous.

The way to destroy vice is to practice its opposite. Since the recovering alcoholic has finely honed vices, the process of vice purgation is hard. When a vice and its corresponding virtue coexist, they do so only for a short time. Eventually, either the vice or virtue will dominate and the other is forfeited. The development of virtue must simultaneously occur with the breaking up of the habits that collectively form vice. The alcoholic's soul is the battleground between the virtue of temperance and the passion of gluttony. When the Holy Spirit reigns inwardly, vices like drunkenness naturally disappear.

Recovering Christian alcoholics should seek the virtues most beneficial to their recovery. They must identify their dominant vice and mercilessly assault it. They must first develop those virtues which would keep them sober and secondly those virtues which would have naturally developed if they did not become drunks. The internal virtue the alcoholic should acquire is temperance and self-denial with the exterior practice of fasting. Temperance is habitual moderation in the indulgence of the appetite, but abstinence when applied to alcohol. Temperance helps subdue all pathological hunger drives including the gluttony for alcohol. The virtue of temperance should be practiced frequently by the Christian alcoholic because the habit of drunkenness was acquired by years of gluttonous gorging on alcohol. The alcoholic who puts restraint on himself will acquire virtue. The practice of peripheral virtues, although inherently good, does not pull the vice out at the roots.

As virtuous acts are continuously practiced they become easier. Eventually they become internalized and the virtue becomes part of the person's character. The acquisition of virtue makes the Christian alcoholic more healthy. It protects them from demonic aggression, their own evil tendencies and relapse. Resistance to temptation develops true virtue. Conflict, adversity, troubles, and pain-these test virtue.

There are many opportunities for the alcoholic to practice virtue. For example, when the recovering alcoholic's spouse dredges up unforgiven behaviors, patience is tested. The alcoholic has to deal with his own anger. If the virtue of patience were present the recovering alcoholic would automatically be at peace when provoked. If they have to wrestle with their emotional response, it is an indication that perfect patience has not yet become an acquired virtue. Eventually, all alcoholics in Christian recovery will realize that they need to develop the virtue of patience.

Virtue is demonstrated by faithfully and consistently performing the little things such as daily resisting temptation, praying, reading scripture, and doing acts of mercy. It is more virtuous to constantly accomplish small things than to occasionally accomplish great things. It is much harder to consistently subordinate inordinate passions and lusts. Almost anyone can muster up enough short-term fortitude for a glorious task. The traveler through a mountain range must walk up and down each mountain step by step. It is painstaking and constant.

## The Pursuit of Christian Perfection

Man, being made in God's image and likeness, was originally created with a degree of perfection that fallen mankind does not possess. While on earth man will never attain heavenly perfection. Neither will he regain the perfection lost by original sin. Being restored to that state that God intended for Adam is unattainable on this side of the grave. God has placed a cap on perfection but even this lower degree of perfection is beyond the ability of most. As fallen children of Adam, we are in an inferior state, and the drunk is far below this state. The drunk would need to grow a thousand fold to ascend even to this inferior state.

Mankind, angels, animals, plants, and even inanimate objects, each have their own degree of perfection in God's eye. The human state of perfection is more noble than that of animals, plants or inanimate objects because his includes godly qualities. Nevertheless, the human mind, will, and emotions remain less than perfect. Man's body is not perfect, not even the healthiest athlete. All get sickness. Man's mind is not perfect. His ability to focus attention and acquire knowledge has profound limits. Man's will is not perfect since it is often hindered by circumstances. Man's emotions are not perfect since he is often feeling bad for no objective reason. Man's spirit is damaged since he commits sin. Christians do not embody perfect faith, hope, love, joy, peace, kindness, or meekness.

Even the holiest person on Earth knows they are not perfect. They are mere mortals scratching out a life while sojourning on earth. The closer they get to perfection the more glaring their remaining imperfections become. It's odd that drunks cannot see their own imperfections, but that is the nature of denial.

Perfection is a noble pursuit and provided the alcoholic's goal is the imitation of Christ, the mere act of trying is perfection. This is because earthly perfection consists in living the process of spiritual progress. When a mortal is on the road of spiritual progress they are actually experiencing what they were created for; continuous closer union with God. Since they are doing what God made them for, as they do it they are perfected. All a mortal can do is go from glory to glory, never attaining an end, since with each new perfection the end becomes more glorious. People are always seeking perfection in outward practices, but it can only be measured by the degree of union with God. It consists of renouncing Satan, self, and the world. Because there is always room for improvement, perfection is not a goal to be achieved, but a process to be lived.

Perfection begins with sobriety for the drunk. The decision to replace the vices of lust, gluttony, laziness, and pleasure seeking with the virtues of self-sacrifice and a commitment for spiritual progress is perfection personified manifesting itself through the holy actions of a creature in living worship of the Creator. Perfection for the alcoholic consists of resisting the demons' ploys in whatever form they appear. When an alcoholic experiences the temptation to drink and resists, he presents himself as a living sacrifice and is being as perfect as man is able.

The process of spiritual perfection can be initiated regardless of the alcoholic's current degree of perfection. It is a long road, which has many milestones, but it begins wherever you start. The saint and the drunk both have the same opportunity for equal progress relative to their state. Although it is relative perfection, God counts it as absolute perfection. The drunk who repents has made progress equal to the saint who does an extraordinary task since both require equal effort. Neither task is more perfect because both cause closer union with God.  The same forward momentum of purging self, demons, and the world is constant regardless of the initial degree of perfection.  They should look upon the mature Christian's great accomplishments and try to duplicate them. They should not be envious of the more mature Christian who, having attained a higher degree of perfection, is able to command acts of spiritual greatness.  Drunks should be rightfully proud because of their sobriety.  This is because repentance from drunkenness is an extraordinary spiritual task. The angels rejoice when drunks repent. The drunk has changed his eternal destiny from hell to Heaven.

The goal of absolute perfection, even though far beyond attainment, needs to be strived for because it draws the alcoholic toward the highest standard.  An extremely high standard causes those who fail to come much closer to the ideal than if they had lower goals. Some people confuse healthy high standards with a vice, which minimizes all accomplishment. Perfectionism is a pathology very common in recovering alcoholics.  Perfectionism will minimize their six months of sobriety.  It causes the alcoholic to believe that their incremental progress is not worth the effort, therefore they relapse.  It places them in the situation of always failing because they never attain unrealistic goals. Horses cannot fly and people cannot be perfect.

## Surrender-Cooperation with Grace

God calls all Christians, but especially the drunks, to freely yield their will to Him.  Surrender means that the drunk made a decision to give up trying to heal himself and instead to cooperate with God's efforts to heal him. In surrender, recovery switches from one's own works to faith in God.  Successful sobriety is based on uniting personal willpower with God's healing grace.  Although the source of the grace is external, once transmitted by God and received by the drunk, it becomes uniquely theirs. This means that it's no longer the drunken alcoholic's willpower that causes sobriety, but their ability to cooperate with God's grace. As the recovering alcoholic begins to cooperate with God's grace, God sees them as a good and faithful servant. He gives them special graces reserved for His children. Without the willful yielding of the will, God is bound by his own word to allow the drunk to do as he pleases regardless of its negative consequences.

The drunk's will for sobriety is so weak that it is incapable of overpowering the inordinate desire to drink. Ironically, even in this weakened state, a frontal assault on the alcoholic's will is futile since its defenses snap into place. When the alcoholic surrenders, the will voluntarily declines to activate its defenses. When faced with an overwhelming enemy, surrender is the reasonable option. The act of surrender is the mechanism that bestows power into the recovering Christian's will. Through infusion of grace they now possess the internal resources to decide to stop being a drunk and remain sober. When willpower is internally generated, the alcoholic's sobriety will be painful and difficult. No wonder- the poor sinner is taking on demons all by himself. When the drunk stops by willpower, only abstinence has any spiritual value. Through surrender the alcoholic has done two things-the cessation of drunkenness and the act of surrender-both of which bring down God's favor.

When drunks surrender their will, the suffering they go through is a genuine living sacrifice, holy and acceptable. It purges the old nature and gives life to the new nature. A transformation takes place in the drunken alcoholic's will. It becomes empowered to throw off the shackles of addiction to embrace victory and peace. The double mindedness of the old nature dies. The intellectual battle ends. The drunk wants to stop drinking but does not yet have the ability. The drunken alcoholic can either cooperate or reject this gift of grace.

The disease dictates that the drunk who stops drinking by willpower will struggle with his craving. For the drunk who surrenders, God usually makes sobriety relatively easy to accomplish. When God is asked to help, His grace not only empowers the will, but also simultaneously reduces the desire to drink. They are hardly tempted to drink alcohol and experience little discomfort. This is a special gift from God to the alcoholic. It allows them to move through recovery with great ease, to reassess their life without the constant desire to drink, to marshal their resources, and accumulate grace. It appears that alcohol was never the serious problem it actually was. Therefore, their chances of success are greatly increased. But because they are in this protected state their opportunity to receive merit is limited because God is taking care of most of the work.

The drunk would not be surrendering his right to exercise free will, to make decisions, or change the direction of events. Surrender does not mean that the alcoholic must give up his own mind, will, and emotions. It means he would give up the perverted, depraved aspects. The drunk who surrenders to God freely decides to give up their pathological "stinking-thinking" for divine direction. They are giving God permission to be the Lord of their life.

Surrender is hard enough but total surrender is virtually impossible. Some alcoholics surrender their life to God as much as within their ability. Partial surrender is the beginning of the spiritual journey. They may genuinely surrender their time, activities, or the right to drink. They may give up riches for ministry. Still, there is one thing they covet, something they unknowingly want and will not surrender. They want to keep the merit, reward, and benefits that God bestows on those that pray, fast, read the Bible, and attend church. Ask them to surrender this and a genuine division rises between those who seek total union versus those who want to maintain their own self.

### Serenity: The Peace of God

After sobriety, peace and serenity is the goal of most recovering alcoholics. In His mercy, God often grants the newly sober Christian alcoholic peace and serenity. This serenity is unmerited grace, because the natural consequences of chronic drunkenness would be negative. In nature instant serenity is out of order but within the spiritual realm, consequences irreconcilable by nature occur often. The serenity functions as a buffer between the environmental stresses and triggers to relapse. God grants serenity because He knows that without this buffer the alcoholic would be a dry drunk or relapse. Serenity is a product of the alcoholic's cooperation with that grace, and what a priceless possession!

Many drunks drink under the mistaken idea that it will give them peace and serenity. For a drunk who drinks three six packs a day, the feeling of peace can be likened to how they feel when they finish their tenth beer. Drunken peace is a transient, drug induced, semi-hypnotic delusional peace. The pseudo-serenity a drunk feels is demonic in origin. The peace the drunk hoped to get from alcohol can never bring true peace. Peace is a fruit of the Holy Spirit granted only by God. The drunk can never attain true peace since this fruit is not granted to those who practice grave sin. This is a manifestation of "stinking thinking" because they seek peace from a bottle, not God.

Alcoholics lose their serenity when they desire anything to an excess. How can the alcoholic, whether drunk or sober, expect any serenity when he or she is craving alcohol? The lust for alcoholic drunkenness makes it impossible for the alcoholic to have serenity.

True serenity is not merely something the recovering alcoholic receives; it is also a source of peace in the world. Some people do not have peace because their presence seems to remove the peace of all whom they encounter. This is the reason that the dry drunk can never experience peace. They are a constant source of contention in the world. They create discord, not peace.

A good conscience is needed in order to attain peace. A troubled mind, the opposite of peacefulness, comes from many things, many of which, like drunkenness, should not be practiced anyway. Once they drink, they become plagued with guilt. This ensures discord. The drunk does not possess peace because he has a guilty conscience. Unless the alcoholic and God are at peace, they can never have peace. Genuine repentance is a prerequisite for internal peace.

Prayer is a way to acquire peace. One reason people in recovery experience excessive anxiety is because they do not pray enough. During a crisis prayer does a lot to alleviate stress, but a prayerful lifestyle prevents internal discord. Fervent prayer, constant prayer, earnest prayer, praying in the spirit; these are all noble pursuits which promote peace. The Christian alcoholic who attends church, Alcoholic's Anonymous meetings, reads the Bible and Twelve Step literature, as well as practices prayer and fasting has the greatest potential to transition into a happy and peaceful sobriety. These spiritual exercises are not the last end but merely the means to the end. Peace is the end, which comes from the practice of these spiritual exercises. At the hour of death the recovering alcoholic will look back and be happy because physical death is much easier to handle when a person has died daily through the practice of spiritual exercises.

There is a difference between worldly peace and spiritual peace. Worldly peace can be found in riches or fame but true Godly peace is never found in these worldly trappings. What does it profit a man to gain the whole world and consequently lose his eternal soul? King Midas had all the gold he wanted but he was miserable. King Richard would have traded his kingdom for a horse. Worldly people, and especially alcoholics, focus on the physical, temporal, sensual, and visual world. They focus their attention on the important people who can improve their own state. True peace is not possible to those who love the world. They cannot achieve peace because they are overly concerned about what others think or say about them.

When the alcoholic trusts in God they can attain peace. Their relationship with God becomes more important than their relationship to the world. Things of the world do not occupy their attention because they are counted as worthless when compared to the things of God. They would rather suffer greatly than separate themselves from God by sin. True serenity must coexist with the enemies of pain, adversity, and tribulation. That is why the spiritually mature are joyful under good or adverse conditions. Things which would make a worldly person get upset are virtually meaningless to the person in union with God. They no longer worry about worldly things that do not affect spiritual things. The spiritually sober alcoholic's focus has changed from self, demons, and the world, to God Almighty. The Christian alcoholic who turns inward and away from the allures of the world is spiritually positioned to receive the peace of God. When recovering alcoholics look to the exterior world for peace they experience anxiety.

Serenity occurs when the alcoholic's only purpose is to love God and to do His will. The more the recovering alcoholic renounces his desire to drink, the more serenity he will acquire. The recovering alcoholic must bring all his passions, desires, and will in submission to God's will and place them under His control. Serenity shrouds those who consistently make decisions consistent with God's will. Once this is accomplished the alcoholic will experience much serenity. After the battle of the wills is over and the drunk has surrendered his life, particularly his drinking, peace and serenity dwell in his soul. They not only surrender their attachment to drunkenness, but they surrender their attachment to themselves. This is a final milestone on the road of spiritual progress. True serenity comes about by losing all attachment to exterior things, but more importantly by losing all attachment to self-love and self will. To give up self-love is beyond even the most noble devout Christian. There is no serenity for the person whose thoughts and feelings are motivated by self-love.

Most alcoholics know the serenity prayer. Interestingly, most do not know that it is an excerpt from a prayer written in the year of our Lord 1065 by St. Francis of Assisi. He called it the "Prayer for Wisdom." The abridged version of the prayer is popular in Twelve Step programs, but it seems that the beginning and end are very helpful for recovery.

"O God, you created all things according to your plan. In this very moment, I know you guide and govern the world. Grant me the serenity to accept the things I cannot change, the courage to change the things I can, and the wisdom to know the difference. I ask this through Christ our Lord. Amen."

# THE HOLY SPIRIT EMPOWERED CHRISTIAN SPONSOR

## The Best Type of Sponsor

Being an ambassador for Christ, the Christian sponsor can exercise Jesus' authority. God empowers them with His Holy Spirit so they can be very effective healers. They are infused with the grace to counsel. They promote the alcoholic's change from self-centered to Christ-centered; from nature to grace. They help the recovering alcoholic improve their spiritual life. The emphasis in Christian sponsoring is to renew and sanctify the recovering alcoholic. Not only are the alcoholic's chances of going to Heaven increased, but while living on earth, their quality of life is improved.

Christian sponsors are very directive with moral issues. They cannot minimize sin. As God's representatives, they must call a sin a sin and not a sickness, disease, or crime, even if the sin is done under impulse, compulsion, or delusion. In non-moral issues which do not increase or decrease the probability of going to heaven or hell, Christian sponsors are not directive. In these cases, they would only be reflective. This is important because alcoholics often irrationally look to their sponsor for direction. They need to learn to think for themselves.

Prayer is an essential part of Christian sponsorship. Sponsors should have strong prayer lives and intercede for those under their spiritual direction. Through the Christian sponsor's intercession, many problems can be cured. They may pray that the alcoholic develops coping skills, that their mind is renewed, or they may bind the demons who cause relapse. The sponsor who intercedes succeeds. Spiritual progress can be greatly enhanced during recovery because the fervent prayer of a righteous sponsor has a lot of therapeutic power.

## Sponsoring the Non-Christian

Unsaved recovering alcoholics usually do not present themselves to a minister for counsel. This is why it is important that Holy Spirit-filled sponsors be available within the alcoholic community. They can minister to the otherwise unreachable. They often attract those non-saved of the world that God has called. Since unsaved alcoholics do not know Jesus as the Lord of their life, the Christian sponsor knows it is not always prudent to use manifest Christian counsel. Initially, discussion of God and the Bible could chase away the unsaved alcoholic. Non-Christians could be reasoned with about their drunkenness according to biblical principles without the mention of God or Bible. The biblical principles of speaking softly to an angry person or avoiding adultery are applicable to both the Christian and non-Christian. Prayer between the sponsor and the recovering alcoholic does not necessarily need to be part of the verbal exchange, but the sponsor should still use all his spiritual gifts to help the alcoholic. The non-Christian alcoholic could actually accept Jesus Christ as his Lord and Savior.

To those who do not know God well enough to seek His consolation, He often speaks to the counselors, sponsors, or spiritual directors from which they seek advice.

There are counseling limitations when sponsoring non-Christians. The primary limitation is that the sponsor must heal without 100 percent of the alcoholic's cognitive cooperation.

## The Danger of Non-Christian Sponsors

The non-Christian sponsor's aversion to Jesus is not surprising since they themselves are unsaved. They do not believe that sin, demons, or witchcraft can cause and/or reinforce alcoholism or drunkenness. They are the blind leading the blind because they are ignorant of the alcoholic's spiritual warfare. They do not have a clue as to the spiritual struggles the recovering Christian alcoholic is going through. The non-Christian sponsor cannot transfer a possession they do not possess. Much of the counsel given by non-Christian sponsors is as grieving to God and entertaining to the demons as when primitive man tried to exorcise demons by cutting a hole in the skull.

Their de-sanctified presence has negative consequences on the recovering alcoholic in this world and the next. The more exposure to this type of sponsor, the more the alcoholic is in need of God's help. After years of direction from a non-Christian sponsor, an alcoholic may spend eternity in hell's fire upon death.

To make a bad situation worse, some sponsors have an occult or new age orientation and advise according to this philosophy. The recovering alcoholic needs Christian solutions to life's problems, not theories of demons and men. Christian direction is not mere theory; it is anointed by God and given power to heal. An occult or new age approach may appear to be beneficial but there would be no forward momentum of grace since new age techniques are all demonic at their core.

Self actualization is the ultimate development an alcoholic can achieve through a non-Christian sponsor. It is the secular parallel to the Christian renewing of the mind, but minus God and holiness. Actualization impedes Christian formation because it reinforces self and the old nature that need to be dead. An alcoholic could become the most actualized person from Adam until the end of time and when they die, they may still go to hell. Many non-Christian sponsors would say that encouraging a patient toward sanctification is not proper sponsorship. Much of what these sponsors practice is a great offense to God. If non-Christian sponsors do not help the alcoholic renew their mind, what are they doing?

Apocrypha reveals that when Jesus was a child He often played with mud like other children. Jesus often molded the mud into statues of birds. He tossed them into the air, gave life to the statues, and they flew away. This power was not beyond Jesus since He transformed dirt into Adam. Concerning the alcoholic, the Christian sponsor is like the child Jesus. The secular sponsor is like the other children playing with mud. The statues of birds they made were mud in the form of a bird, with no life. All they did was reorganize the mud's form. That is what many secular sponsors do, they reorganize the alcoholic's personality without healing the core problem. The most a secular sponsor has to offer is a reorganization of the alcoholic's defensive structure and personality.

## Knowledge Versus Discernment Based Diagnosis

It is a person's philosophy of disease that determines their choice of categories when looking for its cause. Clinical phenomena are perceived differently depending on the observer's viewpoint. Many spiritual diseases and their symptoms are perceived by secular scientific personnel as biological or psychological illness. This is worldly but since they are in the world, they naturally focus on the observable, biological, and psychological aspects of disease. They cannot objectively see, feel, or measure the spiritual realities of cause and effect in illness. These are invisible and non-corporeal until they manifest in the physical realm as illness.

Generally, a medical diagnosis is more objective than a psychological diagnosis. Spiritual diagnosis is often based on the spiritual authority of the minister. Therefore, it is not considered valid or reliable by the scientific community. Ministers perceive the invisible realm and operate within it to a degree not attainable by the average person. The minister's theory of disease baffles them. Since the minister's theory of disease is vastly different, it is reasonable to assume that their diagnostic procedures would be very different. Science does not diagnose spiritual causes because they do not consider them a reality, only the fantasy of religion. They do not follow the diagnostic trail wherever it leads because of pre-conceived notions. If they would do a true differential diagnosis and include the spiritual dimension of man there would be significant healing, especially inside the psychiatric hospitals.

The knowledge-based diagnosis is made by combining education, experience, and natural intuition. Education is the foundation, and experience builds on that foundation. Basically, the knowledge-based diagnosis uses natural methods while the discernment-based diagnosis uses supernatural methods. Both the Christian and non-Christian make knowledge-based diagnoses.

Most people would prefer to go to a sponsor with twenty years of sponsoring experience rather than one who just began recovery. The gift of discernment, powerfully manifested, can make up for twenty years of experience even by a sponsor new to recovery. The sponsor who uses discernment operates on a spiritual level which goes far beyond the skills of the knowledge-based diagnostician. Discernment operates independent of experience and education. Discernment is a powerful gift from God and works in tandem with knowledge.

Diagnosis is much more than finding the cause of a disease and assigning a label. A diagnosis is not complete unless it prescribes the correct treatment. God grants discernment to those He anoints to minister and they supernaturally diagnose and prescribe the correct treatment. The treatment may be deliverance, hope to a depressed person, change of diet, exercise regimen, or referral to the scientific healers.

Discernment is absolutely necessary when the Christian sponsor attempts to discover the spiritual problems underlying alcoholism. Discernment gives the sponsor the ability to distinguish between the subtle attacks of Satan. It is needed to unravel the relationship between the work of the devil and the work of the flesh. The interaction between the spirit, soul, and body regarding drunkenness are very dynamic. Syndromes blend so that identical manifestations sometimes appear to arise from one or any combination of causes. It is difficult enough to distinguish between the physiological and psychological causes of alcoholism. Imagine the difficulty when considering spiritual causes. Only the Holy Spirit can sort through the circular mechanisms that produce the alcoholic. The effects of original sin, personal sin, the sins of others, generational curses, and more direct demonic attacks mysteriously blend to make a true spiritual cause of alcoholism undiagnosable by knowledge. A good diagnostician can usually sort out most illnesses and make a correct diagnosis, but even good diagnosticians occasionally mis-classify.

Discernment is a very deep understanding of God's and Satan's working in an alcoholic. Therefore, only the sponsor who possesses the gift of discernment can definitively diagnose alcoholism. The sponsor who does not possess discernment is at a disadvantage and should pray for the full manifestation of this precious, priceless gift.

### Human Nature

Knowledge. The sponsor knows much about the alcoholic even before they meet. The sponsor knows he will be opposed by "stinking thinking." He knows that each alcoholic is a triune being with a body, soul, and spirit, any of which can be the stronghold for alcoholism. He also knows that the alcoholic is afflicted by original and actual sin, the sins of others, generational curses, and more direct demonic activity. More importantly, the Christian sponsor knows that the alcoholic may be unsaved or a carnal Christian. When sponsoring someone it is imperative to know exactly at which state of being (unsaved or carnal Christian) they are operating on because the alcoholic's level of resistance will vary.

A diagnostic indicator is the disparity between the gifts and fruits of the Holy Spirit. The carnal Christian may instantly possess many free gifts from God, but the fruits of the Holy Spirit are acquired through time, proper living, commitment, surrender to Christ, etc. The degree of disparity determines Christian immaturity. The mature Christian has more congruence between the gifts and fruits.

Discernment. Knowledge of man's triune nature, the manifestation of sin or direct demonic activity, and how these factor into the alcoholic's state of being are necessary but insufficient for effective ministry to the alcoholic. Discernment is necessary because many carnal Christians masquerade as mature, Holy Spirit-filled Christians. It requires discernment to uncover an alcoholic who is merely talking the talk. Discernment is especially necessary when sponsoring non-Christian alcoholics. The unsaved client may have been sent by God to the Christian sponsor for an intervention that would transform them into a Christian. Conversly, discernment teaches when it may be prudent to refer them elsewhere. They could be wasting the Christian sponsor's valuable time throwing pearls to pigs. This determination can only be made by discernment. When the sponsor cannot discern God's will, a soul could be lost.

## Sin

Knowledge. The classification of sin is important for the sponsor because there are different treatment approaches for mortal or venial sin; sin committed ignorantly versus sin committed deliberately; and for willful sin versus sin committed under compulsion. The Christian sponsor can determine the alcoholic's spiritual progress. Direct questioning as well as observation can do much.

Discernment. Discernment is necessary because alcoholics are often secretive about their sinful behaviors and are expert in covering them up. Discernment is necessary because biblically and clinically sin can be a motivation without being an observable act. Jesus said a person could commit adultery without the act being physically consummated. Discernment is also necessary because many alcoholics lack the inferential ability to understand their own sinful state. Possibly denial or delusion blinds them.

Only the gift of discernment will be effective in dealing with this type of alcoholic. Through discernment sponsors have told alcoholics their exact sin in detail. Only then do the alcoholics repent, often stating they wanted to confess their sin but were unable. Once confessed, real healing begins.

## Guilt

Knowledge. We know that man is guilty through his very nature, and through his actions he incurs guilt. When a person is feeling guilty, even the average observer can perceive their guilty countenance.

It is important to make the diagnosis of guilt, but it is more important to be able to diagnose which type of guilt the alcoholic is experiencing in order to provide the correct treatment. The two types of guilt are recorded in 2 Corinthians

7:10 as sorrow. "Godly sorrow brings repentance that leads to salvation and leaves no regret, but worldly sorrow brings death." The sponsor must diagnose whether God or Satan is using the guilt. Acute guilt is from God. This type of guilt is not a problem but rather part of the cure. It will shape behavior into conformity with God's will. It motivates healing. It acts as a catalyst to hinder the alcoholic from repeating a sinful behavior. The sponsor needs to help the alcoholic embrace this guilt and provide strategies to avoid repetition of the sin.

Chronic guilt is not from God. It is a pathological consequence. It is mental bondage and causes the alcoholic to feel depressed or even suicidal. It demoralizes and puts the alcoholic into a state of hopelessness and helplessness. When an alcoholic experiences this type of guilt they are not experiencing God's forgiveness. It destroys their internal resources, which ward off temptation and it increases the probability of relapse.

Discernment. Everyone experiences guilt, but because of psychopathology, not everyone experiences conscious guilt. Others do not have enough character to experience guilt. There are also the perverts who reverse virtue and vice. In order to sort out the bondage that unconscious guilt has on an alcoholic's character, discernment is necessary.

**Forgiveness**

Knowledge. Without discernment the sponsor can determine who the alcoholic needs to forgive by using an interactive prayer. A list of names would be created before the prayer session. The sponsor would lead the alcoholic in prayer and ask God to bless the alcoholic's relatives, teachers, classmates, employers, co-workers, and others on the list. The sponsor would observe whether the patient omits, tenses up when mentioning, or is unable to bless someone on the list.

There is a high probability the alcoholic needs to forgive whomever they exhibit this behavior toward.

Discernment. Some alcoholics say one thing to their sponsor and know something else to be true. They may say they love their parents while secretly they harbor hate because their drunken parents beat them. The sponsor needs to be able to discern the areas in the alcoholic's life that are immobilized by lack of forgiveness. Discernment is necessary in order to sort out which areas the alcoholic needs to experience forgiveness, especially when even the alcoholic is unaware of the need. They may have repressed an incident that needs to be uncovered in order for healing to occur. An alcoholic may have forgotten an offense because it occurred years ago. When a person is not aware of the need to forgive, their subconscious is poisoned and their recovery is hindered. Discernment is necessary to diagnose this problem.

## Treatment for Supernatural Generational Curses

Generational curses are caused by demons, which attach themselves to a family line for successive generations. There is one treatment method with two different procedures, which break supernatural generational curses, neither of which are counseling. The standard treatment method is the deliverance service. The second treatment method stretches the term deliverance to a very drawn out, protracted length. When each new generation progressively imprints the mind of Christ onto its descendants, the demonic influence becomes so negligible the demons decide to leave because they could be more destructive elsewhere. The generational curse is slowly broken through several consecutive generations. Without direct deliverance, many generations are necessary to break a generational curse.

The probability of the curse being transferred to the next generation is dependent on the parents' personal relationship with Jesus. A parent who gets on his knees and prays has done much to break a generational curse as opposed to the parent who gets drunk. Even when a descendent becomes a Christian they appear to always be struggling with alcohol. They go to church, read the Bible, pray, fast, and even loose most of their attachment to drunkenness, yet despite this, they are especially vulnerable to demonic attack through alcohol. These Christians are living under a generational curse, a spiritual stronghold or bondage. The generational curse of alcoholism will reign unchecked unless there are specific, alcohol related Christian interventions.

Generational curses pass something down a family line. Conversion to Christianity does not automatically break them. Upon conversion there is a lot of inner healing but demonic strongholds require extra effort. Often they continue until an individual specifically addresses the sin issue that caused God's curse. The strategy to break a generational curse is to determine the "original sin" which called down God's curse. Then the descendent should personally repent. In addition, they should vicariously repent for their ancestors' sins and personally forgive them for the grief that was generationally transferred. An individual sinner would examine his conscience, confess his sins, and receive God's forgiveness. Although it is more difficult, the victim of a generational curse must do an examination of their family's conscience. The same rules for a personal examination of conscience apply to the family examination of conscience. The person should be boldly thorough. A prayer with specific wording to break the generational curse must be proclaimed and the victim of the curse must forgive those relatives who have caused and perpetuated the curse. This will revoke the legal right to continue the curse. At this point the curse is broken but there may linger a residual effect. Counseling can now be very effective, whereas before the deliverance, it was useless.

## Counseling a Backslider

In order to be a backslider, one must first be a Christian who has rejected the truth, life, and way. The Christian who commits a sin is not a backslider. Many mature Christians commit an occasional sin. Many alcoholics new to recovery initially continue with some alcohol-related sin. Backsliding refers to a lifestyle of sin, not an individual sinful act. If the alcoholic relapsed because of an emotional problem, compulsion, or immaturity then the sponsor should be long suffering. If the alcoholic relapsed with cold-hearted forethought, the sponsor should first confront and rebuke the backslider. If the alcoholic repents he should be forgiven (Luke 17:3). The sponsor should administer forgiveness, grace, and mercy. When the backslider refuses to reestablish recovery the sponsorship relationship should be discontinued. This is the proper treatment for backsliders.

The sober alcoholic has more to be concerned about than whether or not they drink again. Relapse is more than backsliding; it is the second battle in the spiritual war, which they must bravely overcome. Relapse is not merely a night of drunkenness, but it's an opportunity for demons to send the drunk's soul to hell. One relapse, one mortal accident, go to hell.

## Deliverance

Within the Christian community the word deliverance has many meanings. It is used to describe the absence of temptation to which a person was previously a slave. The person released from the sin might say they were delivered.

Deliverance is also used to describe the conversion phenomena, because the person was set free from their old nature. Deliverance is also a synonym for exorcism.

Conversion to Christianity is healing, is salvation, and is deliverance. There is a great change in the new Christian from corruption to perfection. God imprints character traits and their spirit is energized with power to resist temptation.

Self deliverance is the process whereby the Christian struggles with the wiles of the devil and is victorious. It involves resisting temptation, submitting to God's will, fasting, crucifying the flesh, and carrying their cross. It is a process in which a person's sinful nature is peeled off. Over time, the mind sheds self and world to bear the mind of Christ. Self deliverance releases the person from the fetters of sin and allows them to be blessed with the fruit of the Holy Spirit. The double mindedness of the old nature dies and the mind more closely resembles Christ's. When man has the mind of Christ his personality is renewed, healed, sanctified, and blessed. As the mind of Christ is acquired, the disease of alcoholism decreases.

Salvation is done automatically by God upon conversion. Man's part is only to accept Christ, God does the rest. In contrast, through self-deliverance, the Christian defends against and repels demons, which are externally attacking his soul through temptation. The Christian delivers himself, through God's grace, from evil.

Deliverance can be burdensome because the alcoholic is called to do things that require great effort on their part, since they really want to sin, not resist. Self-deliverance hurts. It is not pleasurable in this world. It is a burning fire that takes its toll on the old nature, but gives life to the new nature. The suffering they go through will be a genuine living sacrifice, holy and acceptable. Many Christians are not able to persevere because of this obstacle. For the Christian interested in holiness, sanctification, and renewing, the stress of self-deliverance is less intense, often subliminal. They are supernaturally pulled toward perfection, wanting to leave corruption behind. Self-deliverance purges the old nature.

Prior to salvation alcoholic X was a murderer, sexual pervert, and thief. Upon conversion he instantly transformed into a new creature. He no longer murdered or practiced perversion. To his shame he continued to be a slave to alcoholism and stealing. He discovered that his old sinful behaviors had become undesirable. He found that although he wanted to serve God he often failed and that he did not want to serve Satan but often did. This is the precarious situation of many new Christians. They appear to have one foot in heaven and the other foot in hell.

## Counseling the Alcoholic for Death, Judgment, and Eternity

Death is part of the curse placed on mankind because of the fall of Adam. It is a natural part of life. Except for Enoch (Genesis 5:24) and Elijah (2 Kings 2:11) all have experienced physical death. Even though life on Earth is full of pain and suffering most pathologically cling to this mortal life. They want to live a long life on Earth, even to the delay of Christ's triumphant return. To continue in mortal life many devout Christians would oppose God's will. In response to the hope "maybe Christ will return today," they comment that they hope He does not return today because they have a lot they wish to accomplish. They hold on to their life, and demonstrate that their treasure is here on Earth. This is spiritual absurdity but it is also the human condition.

Other Christians joyfully anticipate the beginning of their life in Heaven. They know they are about to be reunited with loved ones, receive the inheritance and mansion prepared by God, and also be freed from temptation, sin, and other demonic aggression. These Christians do not fear death, although some would admit they fear the method of death. They want to be spared from the pain and suffering of a long and painful terminal illness. The more Christian a terminally ill alcoholic is, the more easily they will accept death. The more attached to the world, the more difficult the acceptance of death will be. Regardless, at the hour of death most people experience a re-evaluation of their life.

Confronted with the diagnosis of terminal illness many alcoholics in recovery choose to bargain with God. They ask to be healed and in return they promise to live a life of ministry. This is a common and valid approach. God has changed His mind based on human petitions. King Hezekiah received fifteen years to his life when at imminent death he vowed to implement God's will in Israel. Science has no notion of the number of spontaneous remissions God implemented in response to prayer.

Actually the person dying of a terminal illness has the distinct advantage over the person who is instantly killed. When instantly killed, the time between death, judgment, and eternity allow no time for repentance. The ill person has time to make themselves right with God. They have an opportunity to wean themselves from the world. They can pursue holiness and sanctification while ill. This is a great opportunity. The sponsor can facilitate this process.

This is a very dangerous time in the alcoholic's life because the temptation to drink usually becomes overwhelming. Twenty years of recovery can be washed away by a tidal wave of booze. Then the drunk dies and goes to hell. Demons mercilessly look for an opportunity to damn recovering alcoholics up until their last hour of life. Demons do not care so much about the process; they just want the outcome to be that the alcoholic's soul rots in hell with them.

Actually drunks are constantly taking definite steps toward death. The effects of alcohol destroy the liver and other body systems. They are more likely to die of accidents. Drunks do not prepare for a good death. At the hour of death, if they are conscious, they have great fear. Their conscience convicts them and they are afraid of God. They regret all the terrible things they did and grieve over all the missed opportunities. They know they are soon to stand before God and be judged for all the evil they did.

In order for the drunk not to fear death he must first repent of his drunkenness. Then he must begin to prepare for his death. He must realize that the drunkenness, which gave him a twisted happiness, will be a cause for severe punishment on the other side of eternity.

# EPILOGUE

Whether I am alive on Earth or in Heaven, the readers of this book are in my prayers. It's not that my prayers are very powerful, but be assured that you have them.

May you continuously transform into the image and likeness of God. May your will more closely conform to God's. May you love God and your neighbor more while loving yourself less. May almighty God have mercy on you, forgive you your sins and bring you to life everlasting. And I bless you in the name of the Father, Son, and Holy Spirit. Amen.